365 Bible Promises for Hurting People

365 BIBLE PROMISES
for Hurting People

A L I C E   C H A P I N

Living Books®
Tyndale House Publishers, Inc.
Wheaton, Illinois

CONTENTS

PREFACE

Suffering is never, never easy. It comes in many forms. Strength ebbs. Mental stress is awful. Sometimes bodies hurt or minds grow dim.

Hurting people need all the help they can get. The suffering ones are often afraid. Some fear pain or isolation or harm for themselves or loved ones. Many feel that nobody cares, that prayers go unheard, or that others have never had it so bad. They wonder why good people suffer.

Scripture promises can make living with hardship and suffering easier. The Bible offers answers to many questions, and it provides comfort we cannot find in other places.

In *365 Bible Promises for Hurting People*, encouraging verses from Scripture are written out, making it easier to claim the appropriate promises and to find God's loving chart through troubled times.

These Scripture selections have been a source of great spiritual strength when my own life's boat seemed to be rocking unmercifully. They have worked time and again to uplift my own spirits and to bring rest, hope, and peace—often in the middle of the night when worry takes over and problems seem bigger than ever. Even while gathering these verses, I often found myself whistling despite turmoil in my own life. Maybe you will too. I like Samuel Rutherford's words of long ago:

> Swim through your temptations and troubles. Run to the promises; they be our Lord's branches hanging over the water so that his half-drowned children may take a grip on them. Let go that grip and you sink to the bottom.

If life is difficult for you right now, if you are hurting in one way or another, this book was written just for you. When you read these carefully chosen Scripture passages and wise sayings of other Christians, I want you to walk away uplifted in spirit and strengthened in mind.

Read and be encouraged and nourished in *your* innermost being!

—ALICE CHAPIN

One

WHEN YOU FEEL AS IF NOBODY CARES

☐ 1 _____

Draw close to God, and God will draw close to you. ❖ No, I will not abandon you as orphans—I will come to you. ❖ God is with those who obey him. ❖ As the deer pants for streams of water, so I long for you, O God. I thirst for God, the living God. (James 4:8; John 14:18; Psalms 14:5; 42:1-2)

TAKEAWAY

Draw close to God, and God will draw close to you.

☐ 2 _____

Not even a sparrow, worth only half a penny, can fall to the ground without your Father knowing it. And the very hairs on your head are all numbered. So don't be afraid; you are more valuable to him than a whole flock of sparrows. (Matthew 10:29-31)

TAKEAWAY
The very hairs on your head are all numbered.

☐ 3 _____

You made all the delicate, inner parts of my body and knit me together in my mother's womb. Thank you for making me so wonderfully complex! Your workmanship is marvelous—and how well I know it. You watched me as I was being formed in utter seclusion, as I was woven together in the dark of the womb. You saw me before I was born. Every day of my life was recorded in your book. Every moment was laid out before a single day had passed. (Psalm 139:13-16)

TAKEAWAY
You made all the delicate, inner parts of my body and knit me together in my mother's womb. You watched me as I was being formed in utter seclusion.

☐ 4 _____

How precious are your thoughts about me, O God! They are innumerable! I can't even count them; they outnumber the grains of sand! And when I wake up in the morning, you are still with me! (Psalm 139:17-18)

When I wake up in the morning, you are still with me!

☐ 5 _____

May your roots go down deep into the soil of God's marvelous love. And may you have the power to understand, as all God's people should, how wide, how long, how high, and how deep his love really is. May you experience the love of Christ, though it is so great you will never fully understand it. Then you will be filled with the fullness of life and power that comes from God. (Ephesians 3:17-19)

TAKEAWAY
May your roots go down deep into the soil of God's marvelous love—it is so great you will never fully understand it.

☐ 6 _____

I will ask the Father, and he will give you another Counselor, who will never leave you. He is the Holy Spirit, who leads into all truth. The world at large cannot receive him, because it isn't looking for him and doesn't recognize him. But you do, because he lives with you now and later will be in you. ❖ Can a mother forget her nursing child? Can she feel no love for a child she has borne? But even if that were possible, I would not forget you! (John 14:15-17; Isaiah 49:15)

**I will ask the Father, and he will give you
another Counselor, who will never leave you.**

□ 7 _____

[Keep your] eyes on Jesus, on whom [y]our faith
depends from start to finish. He was willing to die
a shameful death on the cross. . . . Think about all
he endured when sinful people did such terrible
things to him, so that you don't become weary
and give up. ❖ Since he himself has gone through
suffering and temptation, he is able to help us
when we are being tempted. (Hebrews 12:2-3;
2:18)

T A K E A W A Y
**Since he himself has gone through suffering
and temptation, he is able to help us when we
are being tempted.**

MIND MENDER: As one whom his mother comforteth, so will I comfort you. —Isaiah 66:13, KJV

Two

LORD, I AM AFRAID

□ 8 _____

Be strong and courageous! Do not be afraid or discouraged. For the Lord your God is with you wherever you go. (Joshua 1:9)

TAKEAWAY
The Lord your God is with you wherever you go.

□ 9 _____

God is our refuge and strength, always ready to help in times of trouble. So we will not fear, even if earthquakes come and the mountains crumble into the sea. Let the oceans roar and foam. Let the mountains tremble as the waters surge! ❖ The nations are in an uproar, and kingdoms crumble!

God thunders, and the earth melts! The Lord Almighty is here among us. (Psalm 46:1-3, 6-7)

TAKEAWAY
God is our refuge and strength, always ready to help in times of trouble.

☐ 10 _____

Those who live in the shelter of the Most High will find rest in the shadow of the Almighty. This I declare of the Lord: He alone is my refuge, my place of safety; he is my God, and I am trusting him. ❖ He will shield you with his wings. He will shelter you with his feathers. (Psalm 91:1-2, 4)

TAKEAWAY
Those who live in the shelter of the Most High will find rest in the shadow of the Almighty.

☐ 11 _____

I still belong to you; you are holding my right hand. You will keep on guiding me with your counsel, leading me to a glorious destiny. ❖ My health may fail, and my spirit may grow weak, but God remains the strength of my heart; he is mine forever. . . . How good it is to be near God! I have made the Sovereign Lord my shelter. (Psalm 73:23-24, 26-28)

TAKEAWAY
You are holding my right hand!

☐ 12 _____

This is what the Lord says: Do not be afraid! . . .
for the battle is not yours, but God's. ❖ That is
why we can say with confidence, The Lord is my
helper, so I will not be afraid. What can mere mortals do to me? ❖ What can we say about such wonderful things as these? If God is for us, who can
ever be against us? (2 Chronicles 20:15; Hebrews
13:6; Romans 8:31)

T A K E A W A Y
The battle is not yours, but God's.

☐ 13 _____

Don't be afraid, for I am with you. Do not be dismayed, for I am your God. I will strengthen you. I
will help you. I will uphold you with my victorious right hand. ❖ What is impossible from a
human perspective is possible with God. ❖ In him
lie hidden all the treasures of wisdom and knowledge. (Isaiah 41:10; Luke 18:27; Colossians 2:3)

T A K E A W A Y
**What is impossible from a human perspective is
possible with God.**

☐ 14 _____

You are my strength; I wait for you to rescue me,
for you, O God, are my place of safety. In his
unfailing love, my God will come and help me.
❖ But as for me, I will sing about your power. I
will shout with joy each morning because of

your unfailing love. For you have been my refuge, a place of safety in the day of distress.
(Psalm 59:9-10, 16)

T A K E A W A Y
**In his unfailing love, my God will come and
help me.**

MIND MENDER: Thanks be to God, who in Christ
always leads us in triumph.

Such is the confidence that we have through Christ
toward God. . . . Our sufficiency is from God.
—2 Corinthians 2:14; 3:4-5, RSV

Three

O DEATH, WHERE IS THY STING?

☐ 15 _____

The Lord's loved ones are precious to him; it grieves him when they die. ❖ For this world is not our home; we are looking forward to our city in heaven, which is yet to come. (Psalm 116:15; Hebrews 13:14)

TAKEAWAY
We are looking forward to our city in heaven, which is yet to come.

☐ 16 _____

We wish you not to remain in ignorance, brothers, about those who sleep in death; you should not grieve like the rest of men, who have no hope. We believe that Jesus died and rose again; and so it

will be for those who died as Christians; God will
bring them to life with Jesus. (1 Thessalonians
4:13-14, NEB)

TAKEAWAY
The thief who repented on the cross next to
Jesus' cross was told that within that very day,
he would be with Jesus in paradise.

☐ 17 _____

But now God has shown us a different way of
being right in his sight—not by obeying the law
but by the way . . . we are made right in God's
sight when we trust in Jesus Christ to take away
our sins. And we all can be saved in this same
way, no matter who we are or what we have
done. ❖ For God sent Jesus to take the punishment for our sins and to satisfy God's anger
against us. We are made right with God when
we believe that Jesus shed his blood, sacrificing
his life for us. God was being entirely fair and
just when he did not punish those who sinned
in former times. ❖ Can we boast, then, that we
have done anything to be accepted by God? No,
because our acquittal is not based on our good
deeds. It is based on our faith. So we are made
right with God through faith and not by obeying the law. (Romans 3:21-22, 25, 27-28)

TAKEAWAY
We are made right in God's sight when we trust
in Jesus Christ to take away our sins—no matter
who we are or what we have done.

This is what God has testified: He has given us eternal life, and this life is in his Son. So whoever has God's Son has life; whoever does not have his Son does not have life. I write this to you who believe in the Son of God, so that you may know you have eternal life. (1 John 5:11-13)

TAKEAWAY

Whoever has God's Son has life.

Don't be troubled. You trust God, now trust in me. There are many rooms in my Father's home, and I am going to prepare a place for you. If this were not so, I would tell you plainly. When everything is ready, I will come and get you, so that you will always be with me where I am. (John 14:1-3)

TAKEAWAY

There are many rooms in my Father's home, and I am going to prepare a place for you. You will always be with me where I am.

> *My knowledge of that life is small,*
> *The eye of faith is dim;*
> *But 'tis enough that Christ knows all*
> *And I shall be with him.*
>
> —RICHARD BAXTER

Since Christ lives within you, even though your body will die because of sin, your spirit is alive because you have been made right with God. The Spirit of God, who raised Jesus from the dead, lives in you. And just as he raised Christ from the dead, he will give life to your mortal body by this same Spirit living within you. (Romans 8:10-11)

T A K E A W A Y

He will give life to your mortal body by this same Spirit living within you.

□ 21

For God has reserved a priceless inheritance for his children. It is kept in heaven for you, pure and undefiled, beyond the reach of change and decay. And God, in his mighty power, will protect you until you receive this salvation, because you are trusting him. It will be revealed on the last day for all to see. ❖ Then Jesus shouted, "Father, I entrust my spirit into your hands!" And with those words he breathed his last. (1 Peter 1:4-5; Luke 23:46)

T A K E A W A Y

God has reserved a priceless inheritance for his children. God, in his mighty power, will protect you until you receive this salvation.

MIND MENDER: The Scripture says there is a time to be born and a time to die. And when my time to die comes, an angel will be there to comfort me. He will give me peace and joy even at the most critical hour, and usher me into the presence of God, and I will dwell with the Lord forever. Thank God for the ministry of His blessed angels! —Billy Graham, *Angels: God's Secret Agents*

General "Stonewall" Jackson was a dedicated Christian who loved his church and taught Sunday school. Jackson distributed Bibles to his men, directed worship services in his military camps, and openly paused for prayer two or three times daily. As General Robert E. Lee's right-hand man, he faced death nearly every day during the Civil War years. "His field dispatches, official reports, and home correspondence all contained references to 'the blessings of God' and 'an all-wise Providence,'" reports Jackson authority Dr. James I. Robertson Jr. General Jackson's deep faith and quiet devotion motivated and sustained him and those around him through America's bloodiest war. He said, "I do not concern myself about death, but to always be ready, no matter when it may overtake me." He was heard to say he hoped that when "called home" by death, it would be on the Lord's Day. Sure enough, the Lord did call him on a Sunday afternoon, May 10, 1863, at a Virginia railroad crossing following his accidental wounding at the Battle of Chancellorsville. His final words were, "Let us cross over the river and rest under the shade of the trees."

Four

BIBLE PRAYERS

☐ 22 _____

Lord, don't hold back your tender mercies from me. My only hope is in your unfailing love and faithfulness. ❖ Have compassion on me, Lord, for I am weak. Heal me, Lord, for my body is in agony. I am sick at heart. How long, O Lord, until you restore me? Return, O Lord, and rescue me. Save me because of your unfailing love. ❖ Why am I discouraged? Why so sad? I will put my hope in God! I will praise him again—my Savior and my God! (Psalms 40:11; 6:2-4; 42:5-6)

TAKEAWAY
I will praise him again—my Savior and my God!

☐ 23 _____

I am worn out from sobbing. Every night tears drench my bed; my pillow is wet from weeping.

My vision is blurred by grief; my eyes are worn out because of all my enemies. ❖ Hear my prayer, O Lord! Listen to my cries for help! Don't ignore my tears. For I am your guest—a traveler passing through, as my ancestors were before me. ❖ Let me live so I can praise you, and may your laws sustain me. (Psalms 6:6-7; 39:12-13; 119:175)

TAKEAWAY
Let me live so I can praise you.

□ 24 _____

I hear the tumult of the raging seas as your waves and surging tides sweep over me. Through each day the Lord pours his unfailing love upon me, and through each night I sing his songs, praying to God who gives me life. ❖ Why am I discouraged? Why so sad? I will put my hope in God! I will praise him again—my Savior and my God! (Psalm 42:7-8, 11)

TAKEAWAY
Why am I discouraged? Why so sad? I will put my hope in God!

□ 25 _____

I will praise the Lord at all times. I will constantly speak his praises. I will boast only in the Lord; let all who are discouraged take heart. ❖ Oh, the joys of those who trust in him! (Psalm 34:1-2, 8)

TAKEAWAY
I will praise the Lord at all times.

Come, let us tell of the Lord's greatness; let us exalt his name together. ❖ For the angel of the Lord guards all who fear him, and he rescues them. Taste and see that the Lord is good. ❖ He is our God. We are the people he watches over, the sheep under his care. ❖ O Lord my God, you have done many miracles for us. Your plans for us are too numerous to list. (Psalms 34:3, 7-8; 95:7; 40:5)

TAKEAWAY

O Lord my God, you have done many miracles for us.

Your unfailing love is better to me than life itself; how I praise you! I will honor you as long as I live, lifting up my hands to you in prayer. ❖ I lie awake thinking of you, meditating on you through the night. I think how much you have helped me; I sing for joy in the shadow of your protecting wings. ❖ Praise the Lord! Praise the Lord from the heavens! Praise him from the skies! Praise him, all his angels! Praise him, all the armies of heaven! Praise him, sun and moon! Praise him, all you twinkling stars! (Psalms 63:3-4, 6-7; 148:1-3)

TAKEAWAY

I sing for joy in the shadow of your protecting wings. Praise the Lord!

The Lord is my strength, my shield from every danger. ❖ Praise him, skies above! Praise him, vapors high above the clouds! Let every created thing give praise to the Lord. ❖ Praise the Lord from the earth, you creatures of the ocean depths, fire and hail, snow and storm, wind and weather that obey him, mountains and all hills, fruit trees and all cedars, . . . kings of the earth and all people, rulers and judges of the earth, young men and maidens, old men and children. Let them all praise the name of the Lord. For his name is very great; his glory towers over the earth and heaven! (Psalms 28:7; 148:4-5, 7-13)

T A K E A W A Y
The Lord is my strength, my shield from every danger.

MIND MENDER: We forget that God, and only God, the God who loves us so much, knows what he does with our prayers or with anything else. God hears *all* of our prayers. Not only that, he *answers* all of them, in his own time and his own way.

Five

GOD'S LOVE FEELS
SO GOOD

☐ 29 _____

The Lord is like a father to his children, tender
and compassionate to those who fear him. ❖ He
heals the brokenhearted, binding up their
wounds. ❖ He will feed his flock like a shepherd.
He will carry the lambs in his arms, holding them
close to his heart. He will gently lead the mother
sheep with their young. (Psalms 103:13; 147:3;
Isaiah 40:11)

T A K E A W A Y
**The Lord is like a father to his children, tender
and compassionate to those who fear him.**

☐ 30 _____

God the Father chose you long ago, and the Spirit
has made you holy. . . . for it is by his boundless

mercy that God has given us the privilege of being born again. Now we live with a wonderful expectation because Jesus Christ rose again from the dead. ❖ See how very much our heavenly Father loves us, for he allows us to be called his children, and we really are! But the people who belong to this world don't know God, so they don't understand that we are his children. Yes, dear friends, we are already God's children. (1 Peter 1:2-3; 1 John 3:1-2)

TAKEAWAY
God the Father chose you long ago.

☐ 31 _____

Furthermore, because of Christ, we have received an inheritance from God, for he chose us from the beginning, and all things happen just as he decided long ago. God's purpose was that we who were the first to trust in Christ should praise our glorious God. (Ephesians 1:11-12)

TAKEAWAY
We who were the first to trust in Christ should praise our glorious God.

☐ 32 _____

Can anything ever separate us from Christ's love? Does it mean he no longer loves us if we have trouble or calamity, or are persecuted, or are hungry or cold or in danger or threatened with death? ❖ And I am convinced that nothing

can ever separate us from his love. Death can't,
and life can't. The angels can't, and the demons
can't. Our fears for today, our worries about
tomorrow, and even the powers of hell can't
keep God's love away. (Romans 8:35, 38)

TAKEAWAY

**I am convinced that nothing can ever separate
us from his love.—St. Paul**

☐ 33 _____

Your unfailing love, O Lord, is as vast as the heavens. . . . How precious is your unfailing love,
O God! All humanity finds shelter in the shadow
of your wings. ❖ Nothing in all creation will ever
be able to separate us from the love of God that is
revealed in Christ Jesus our Lord. (Psalm 36:5-7;
Romans 8:39)

TAKEAWAY

**Your unfailing love, O Lord, is as vast as the
heavens.**

☐ 34 _____

So you should not be like cowering, fearful slaves.
You should behave instead like God's very own
children, adopted into his family—calling him
"Father, dear Father." For his Holy Spirit speaks to
us deep in our hearts and tells us that we are
God's children. And since we are his children, we
will share his treasures—for everything God gives
to his Son, Christ, is ours, too. (Romans 8:15-17)

You should not be like cowering, fearful slaves. You should behave instead like God's very own children.

☐ 35 _____

I pray that your hearts will be flooded with light so that you can understand the wonderful future he has promised to those he called. I want you to realize what a rich and glorious inheritance he has given to his people. (Ephesians 1:18)

TAKEAWAY
What a rich and glorious inheritance [God] has given to his people.

MIND MENDER: Would you know our Lord's meaning in this thing? Know it well: Love was His meaning. Who showed it you? Love. What did he show you? Love. Why did he show it? For Love. —Julian of Norwich, *Revelations of Divine Love*

Six

I WILL PRAISE GOD ANYWAY

☐ 36 _____

I am God, your God! ❖ All the animals of the forest are mine, and I own the cattle on a thousand hills. Every bird of the mountains and all the animals of the field belong to me. ❖ I don't need the bulls you sacrifice. . . . What I want instead is your true thanks to God. . . . Trust me in your times of trouble, and I will rescue you, and you will give me glory. (Psalm 50:7, 10-11, 13-15)

TAKEAWAY
Trust me in your times of trouble, and I will rescue you, and you will give me glory.

Let them all praise the name of the Lord. For his name is very great; his glory towers over the earth and heaven! ❖ Praise the Lord! Praise God in his heavenly dwelling; praise him in his mighty heaven! Praise him for his mighty works; praise his unequaled greatness! Praise him with a blast of the trumpet; praise him with the lyre and harp! Praise him with the tambourine and dancing; praise him with stringed instruments and flutes! Praise him with a clash of cymbals; praise him with loud clanging cymbals. Let everything that lives sing praises to the Lord! Praise the Lord! (Psalms 148:13; 150:1-6)

TAKEAWAY

Let everything that lives sing praises to the Lord! Praise the Lord!

I waited patiently for the Lord to help me, and he turned to me and heard my cry. He lifted me out of the pit of despair, out of the mud and the mire. He set my feet on solid ground and steadied me as I walked along. He has given me a new song to sing, a hymn of praise to our God. Many will see what he has done and be astounded. They will put their trust in the Lord. (Psalm 40:1-3)

TAKEAWAY

He set my feet on solid ground and steadied me as I walked along.

O Lord my God, I cried out to you for help, and
you restored my health. You brought me up from
the grave, O Lord. You kept me from falling into
the pit of death. Sing to the Lord, all you godly
ones! Praise his holy name. ❖ You have turned
my mourning into joyful dancing. You have taken
away my clothes of mourning and clothed me
with joy, that I might sing praises to you and not
be silent. O Lord my God, I will give you thanks
forever! (Psalm 30:2-4, 11-12)

TAKEAWAY

**You have clothed me with joy, that I might sing
praises to you and not be silent.**

Now unto the King eternal, immortal, invisible,
the only wise God, be honour and glory for ever
and ever. ❖ The Lord reigneth; let the earth
rejoice; let the multitude of isles be glad thereof.
❖ The heavens declare his righteousness, and all
the people see his glory. ❖ Thou, Lord, art high
above all the earth: Thou art exalted far above all
gods. (1 Timothy 1:17; Psalm 97:1, 6, 9, KJV)

TAKEAWAY

**We walk by faith, not by sight. Although the fig
tree shall not blossom . . . yet I will rejoice in
the Lord. (2 Corinthians 5:7; Habakkuk 3:17-
18, KJV)**

_____

My heart is confident in you, O God; no wonder I can sing your praises! Wake up, my soul! Wake up, O harp and lyre! I will waken the dawn with my song. I will thank you, Lord, in front of all the people. I will sing your praises among the nations. For your unfailing love is higher than the heavens. Your faithfulness reaches to the clouds. Be exalted, O God, above the highest heavens. May your glory shine over all the earth. ❖ But you are always the same; your years never end. The children of your people will live in security. Their children's children will thrive in your presence. (Psalms 108:1-5; 102:27-28)

TAKEAWAY

Herein is joy, amid the ebb and flow of the passing world: our God remains unmoved, and His throne endures forever. —Robert Coleman, *Songs of Heaven*

_____

Give thanks to the Lord, for he is good!
   His faithful love endures forever.
Give thanks to the God of gods.
   His faithful love endures forever.
Give thanks to the Lord of lords.
   His faithful love endures forever.
Give thanks to him who alone does mighty
      miracles.
   His faithful love endures forever.

Give thanks to him who made the heavens so
  skillfully.
  His faithful love endures forever.
Give thanks to him who placed the earth on the
  water.
  His faithful love endures forever.
Give thanks to him who made the heavenly
  lights—
  His faithful love endures forever.
The sun to rule the day,
  His faithful love endures forever.
and the moon and stars to rule the night.
  His faithful love endures forever.

  (Psalm 136:1-9)

TAKEAWAY

**Imagine your worst problem. Think of the worst
scenario. Got it in mind? Now, imagine you and
the God of the universe (who made you and
who hurled the planets into space) tackling it
together. Is there anything you and he can't
handle as a team?**

  Night is drawing nigh.
  For all that has been—Thanks!
  For all that shall be—Yes!

  —DAG HAMMARSKJÖLD, *Markings*

Seven

LIVING WITH YOUR HURT

□ 43 _____

I know the Lord is always with me. I will not be shaken, for he is right beside me. ❖ For we know that when this earthly tent we live in is taken down—when we die and leave these bodies—we will have a home in heaven, an eternal body made for us by God himself and not by human hands. ❖ Give thanks to the Lord, for he is good! His faithful love endures forever. (Acts 2:25; 2 Corinthians 5:1; Psalm 118:29)

TAKEAWAY

I know the Lord is always with me. I will not be shaken.

Dear brothers and sisters, you are foreigners and aliens here. So I warn you to keep away from evil desires because they fight against your very souls. ❖ Yet what we suffer now is nothing compared to the glory he will give us later. For all creation is waiting eagerly for that future day when God will reveal who his children really are. Against its will, everything on earth was subjected to God's curse. All creation anticipates the day when it will join God's children in glorious freedom from death and decay. For we know that all creation has been groaning as in the pains of childbirth right up to the present time. (1 Peter 2:11; Romans 8:18-22)

TAKEAWAY

You are foreigners and aliens here. What we suffer now is nothing compared to the glory [God] will give us later.

The name of the Lord is a strong fortress; the godly run to him and are safe. ❖ The Lord is a jealous God, filled with vengeance and wrath. He takes revenge on all who oppose him and furiously destroys his enemies! ❖ The Lord is good. When trouble comes, he is a strong refuge. And he knows everyone who trusts in him. (Proverbs 18:10; Nahum 1:2, 7)

TAKEAWAY

The Lord is good. When trouble comes, he is a strong refuge.

But to keep me from getting puffed up, I was given a thorn in my flesh, a messenger from Satan to torment me and keep me from getting proud. Three different times I begged the Lord to take it away. Each time he said, "My gracious favor is all you need. My power works best in your weakness." So now I am glad to boast about my weaknesses, so that the power of Christ may work through me. . . . For when I am weak, then I am strong. (2 Corinthians 12:7-10)

TAKEAWAY

My gracious favor is all you need. My power works best in your weakness.

For I can do everything with the help of Christ who gives me the strength I need. (Philippians 4:13)

TAKEAWAY

Christ gives me the strength I need.

And now, just as you accepted Christ Jesus as your Lord, you must continue to live in obedience to him. Let your roots grow down into him and draw up nourishment from him, so you will grow in faith, strong and vigorous in the truth you were taught. Let your lives overflow with thanksgiving for all he has done. (Colossians 2:6-7)

Just as you accepted Christ Jesus as your Lord, you must continue to live in obedience to him.

☐ 49 _____

[Lord, when] doubts filled my mind, your comfort gave me renewed hope and cheer. ❖So be strong and take courage, all you who put your hope in the Lord! ❖A cheerful heart is good medicine, but a broken spirit saps a person's strength. ❖Hope deferred makes the heart sick. (Psalms 94:19; 31:24; Proverbs 17:22; 13:12)

T A K E A W A Y

A cheerful heart is good medicine. So be strong and take courage, all you who put your hope in the Lord!

MIND MENDER: He understands my agony. He's been there.

Eight

LORD, I AM GOING TO PRAY MY WAY THROUGH

☐ 50 _____

Confess your sins to each other and pray for each other so that you may be healed. The earnest prayer of a righteous person has great power and wonderful results. ❖ My heart is confident in you, O God; no wonder I can sing your praises! (James 5:16; Psalm 57:7)

TAKEAWAY

The earnest prayer of a righteous person has great power and wonderful results.

☐ 51 _____

Are any among you suffering? They should keep on praying about it. And those who have reason to be thankful should continually sing praises to the Lord. ❖ I urge you, first of all, to pray for all people. As you make your requests, plead for God's mercy upon them, and give thanks. (James 5:13; 1 Timothy 2:1)

Pray for all people. As you make your requests, plead for God's mercy upon them, and give thanks.

☐ 52 _____

Are any among you sick? They should call for the elders of the church and have them pray over them, anointing them with oil in the name of the Lord. And their prayer offered in faith will heal the sick, and the Lord will make them well. And anyone who has committed sins will be forgiven. (James 5:14-15)

TAKEAWAY
Are any among you sick? They should call for the elders of the church and have them pray over them, anointing them with oil in the name of the Lord.

☐ 53 _____

Don't worry about anything; instead, pray about everything. Tell God what you need, and thank him for all he has done. If you do this, you will experience God's peace, which is far more wonderful than the human mind can understand. His peace will guard your hearts and minds as you live in Christ Jesus. (Philippians 4:6-7)

TAKEAWAY
Tell God what you need, and thank him for all he has done. His peace will guard your hearts and minds as you live in Christ Jesus.

☐ 54 _____

Elijah was as human as we are, and yet when he prayed earnestly that no rain would fall, none fell for the next three and a half years! Then he prayed for rain, and down it poured. The grass turned green, and the crops began to grow again. (James 5:17-18)

TAKEAWAY

When Elijah prayed earnestly that no rain would fall, none fell for the next three and a half years!

☐ 55 _____

I love the Lord because he hears and answers my prayers. Because he bends down and listens, I will pray as long as I have breath! (Psalm 116:1-2)

TAKEAWAY

The Lord bends down and listens.

☐ 56 _____

The Holy Spirit helps us in our distress. For we don't even know what we should pray for, nor how we should pray. But the Holy Spirit prays for us with groanings that cannot be expressed in words. And the Father who knows all hearts knows what the Spirit is saying, for the Spirit pleads for us believers in harmony with God's own will. (Romans 8:26-27)

TAKEAWAY

We don't even know what we should pray for. But the Holy Spirit prays for us with groanings that cannot be expressed in words.

MIND MENDER: Some answers come only through fervent prayer. If we are deprived of every capability except a sound mind, if we are illiterate, blind, deaf, even completely paralyzed, we can still be used by God to "stand in the gap," praying into existence a mighty supernatural power unbeknown to most of the world, that alters people, events, even nations. —Anonymous

Nine

SPECIAL PROMISES FOR SENIOR CITIZENS

☐ 57 _____

Listen to me, all you who are left in Israel. I created you and have cared for you since before you were born. I will be your God throughout your lifetime—until your hair is white with age. I made you, and I will care for you. I will carry you along and save you. (Isaiah 46:3-4)

TAKEAWAY
I will be your God throughout your lifetime. I made you, and I will care for you.

☐ 58 _____

You will keep on guiding me with your counsel, leading me to a glorious destiny. ❖ Surely your goodness and unfailing love will pursue me all the days of my life, and I will live in the house of the Lord forever. (Psalms 73:24; 23:6)

TAKEAWAY

You will keep on guiding me with your counsel, leading me to a glorious destiny.

☐ 59 _____

Whom have I in heaven but you? I desire you more than anything on earth. My health may fail, and my spirit may grow weak, but God remains the strength of my heart; he is mine forever. ❖ But as for me, how good it is to be near God! I have made the Sovereign Lord my shelter. (Psalm 73:25-26, 28)

TAKEAWAY

My health may fail, and my spirit may grow weak, but God remains the strength of my heart.

☐ 60 _____

O Lord, you alone are my hope. I've trusted you, O Lord, from childhood. Yes, you have been with me from birth; from my mother's womb you have cared for me. No wonder I am always praising you! My life is an example to many, because you have been my strength and protection. ❖ Even when I walk through the dark valley of death, I will not be afraid, for you are close beside me. Your rod and your staff protect and comfort me. (Psalms 71:5-8; 23:4)

I've trusted you, O Lord, from childhood. From my mother's womb you have cared for me. No wonder I am always praising you!

☐ 61 _____

But I will keep on hoping for you to help me; I will praise you more and more. I will tell everyone about your righteousness. All day long I will proclaim your saving power, for I am overwhelmed by how much you have done for me. I will praise your mighty deeds, O Sovereign Lord. I will tell everyone that you alone are just and good. ❖Now that I am old and gray, do not abandon me, O God. Let me proclaim your power to this new generation, your mighty miracles to all who come after me. Your righteousness, O God, reaches to the highest heavens. You have done such wonderful things. Who can compare with you, O God? (Psalm 71:14-16, 18-19)

Let me proclaim your power to this new generation. Your righteousness, O God, reaches to the highest heavens.

☐ 62 _____

Gray hair is a crown of glory; it is gained by living a godly life. ❖But the godly will flourish like palm trees and grow strong like the cedars of Lebanon. For they are transplanted into the Lord's own house. They flourish in the courts of our God.

Even in old age they will still produce fruit; they will remain vital and green. They will declare, "The Lord is just! He is my rock! There is nothing but goodness in him!" ❖ For that is what God is like. He is our God forever and ever, and he will be our guide until we die. (Proverbs 16:31; Psalms 92:12-15; 48:14)

TAKEAWAY
He is our God forever and ever, and he will be our guide until we die.

☐ 63 _____

When people live to be very old, let them rejoice in every day of life. ❖ Bless the Lord . . . who lives forever from eternal ages past. Amen and amen! (Ecclesiastes 11:8; Psalm 41:13)

TAKEAWAY
When people live to be very old, let them rejoice in every day of life.

MIND MENDER: There is no need to plead that the love of God shall fill our hearts as though He were unwilling to fill us. He is willing as light is willing to flood a room that is opened to its brightness. Willing as water is to flow into an empty channel. Love is pressing around us on all sides like air. Cease to resist it and instantly love takes possession. —Amy Carmichael

It is not how many years we live, but what we do with them. —Evangeline Booth

Ten

STRENGTH IN WEAKNESS

□ 64 _____

If we are unfaithful, he remains faithful, for he cannot deny himself. (2 Timothy 2:13)

TAKEAWAY
If we are unfaithful, he remains faithful.

□ 65 _____

Christ is not weak in his dealings with you; he is a mighty power among you. (2 Corinthians 13:3)

TAKEAWAY
Christ is a mighty power among you.

□ 66 _____

Now glory be to God! By his mighty power at work within us, he is able to accomplish infinitely more than we would ever dare to ask or hope.

May he be given glory in the church and in Christ
Jesus forever and ever through endless ages.
(Ephesians 3:20-21)

TAKEAWAY
**He is able to accomplish infinitely more than
we would ever dare to ask or hope.**

☐ 67 _____

I pray that you will begin to understand the incredible greatness of his power for us who believe him.
This is the same mighty power that raised Christ
from the dead and seated him in the place of honor
at God's right hand in the heavenly realms. Now he
is far above any ruler or authority or power or leader
or anything else in this world or in the world to
come. ❖[Christ] fills everything everywhere with
his presence. (Ephesians 1:19-21, 23)

TAKEAWAY
**His power for us who believe him is the same
mighty power that raised Christ from the dead.**

☐ 68 _____

On the very day I call to you for help, my enemies
will retreat. This I know: God is on my side.
O God, I praise your word. Yes, Lord, I praise your
word. I trust in God, so why should I be afraid?
What can mere mortals do to me? I will . . . offer a
sacrifice of thanks for your help. (Psalm 56:9-12)

TAKEAWAY
This I know: God is on my side.

□ 69 _____

Be strong with the Lord's mighty power. ❖He
alone is my rock and my salvation, my fortress
where I will not be shaken. My salvation and my
honor come from God alone. (Ephesians 6:10;
Psalm 62:6-7)

TAKEAWAY
**My salvation and my honor come from God
alone.**

□ 70 _____

I love you, Lord; you are my strength. ❖But in my
distress I cried out to the Lord; yes, I prayed to my
God for help. He heard me from his sanctuary;
my cry reached his ears. Then the earth quaked
and trembled; the foundations of the mountains
shook. . . . He opened the heavens and came
down. . . . Mounted on a mighty angel, he flew,
soaring on the wings of the wind. . . . The bril-
liance of his presence broke through the clouds,
raining down hail and burning coals. ❖He
reached down from heaven and rescued me; he
drew me out of deep waters. He delivered me
from my powerful enemies. . . . They attacked me
at a moment when I was weakest, but the Lord
upheld me. He led me to a place of safety; he rescued me because he delights in me. (Psalm 18:1,
6-12, 16-19)

He reached down from heaven and rescued me. At a moment when I was weakest, the Lord upheld me.

MIND MENDER: O Lord God Almighty! Where is there anyone as mighty as you, Lord? Faithfulness is your very character. You are the one who rules the oceans. When their waves rise in fearful storms, you subdue them. . . . The heavens are yours, and the earth is yours; everything in the world is yours—you created it all. You created north and south. Mount Tabor and Mount Hermon praise your name. Powerful is your arm! Strong is your hand! Your right hand is lifted high in glorious strength. —Psalm 89:8-13

Eleven

LORD, MY BODY HURTS SO BAD

☐ 71 _____

When you go through deep waters and great trouble, I will be with you. When you go through rivers of difficulty, you will not drown! When you walk through the fire of oppression, you will not be burned up; the flames will not consume you. (Isaiah 43:2)

TAKEAWAY
When you go through deep waters and great trouble, I will be with you.

☐ 72 _____

And even we Christians, although we have the Holy Spirit within us as a foretaste of future glory, also groan to be released from pain and suffering. We, too, wait anxiously for that day when God will give us our full rights as his children, including the new bodies he has promised us. ❖ Be careful! Take a firm stand against [Satan], and be strong in your faith. Remember that Christians all over the world are going through the same kind of suffering you are. (Romans 8:23; 1 Peter 5:8-9)

TAKEAWAY
We wait anxiously for that day when God will give us bodies that will never be sick again and will never die.

☐ 73 _____

For we know that when this earthly tent we live in is taken down—when we die and leave these bodies—we will have a home in heaven, an eternal body made for us by God himself and not by human hands. We grow weary in our present bodies and we long for the day when we will put on our heavenly bodies like new clothing. Our dying bodies make us groan and sigh. (2 Corinthians 5:1-4)

TAKEAWAY
We will have an eternal body made for us by God himself.

☐ 74 _____

It is the same way for the resurrection of the dead. Our earthly bodies, which die and decay, will be different when they are resurrected, for they will never die. Our bodies now disappoint us, but when they are raised, they will be full of glory. They are weak now, but when they are raised, they will be full of power. They are natural human bodies now, but when they are raised, they will be spiritual bodies. ❖When this happens then at last the Scriptures will come true: "Death is swallowed up in victory." O death, where is your victory? O death, where is your sting? (1 Corinthians 15:42-44, 54-55)

TAKEAWAY

When our bodies are raised, they will be full of glory. O death, where is your victory? Where is your sting?

☐ 75 _____

Jesus returned to the Sea of Galilee and climbed a hill and sat down. A vast crowd brought him the lame, blind, crippled, mute, and many others with physical difficulties, and they laid them before Jesus. And he healed them all. The crowd was amazed! Those who hadn't been able to speak were talking, the crippled were made well, the lame were walking around, and those who had been blind could see again! ❖Jesus Christ is the same yesterday, today, and forever. (Matthew 15:29-31; Hebrews 13:8)

TAKEAWAY
He healed them all.

But someone may ask, "How will the dead be raised? What kind of bodies will they have?" When you put a seed into the ground, it doesn't grow into a plant unless it dies first. And what you put in the ground is not the plant that will grow, but only a dry little seed of wheat or whatever it is you are planting. Then God gives it a new body—just the kind he wants it to have. ❖ God himself has prepared us for this, and as a guarantee he has given us his Holy Spirit. (1 Corinthians 15:35-38; 2 Corinthians 5:5)

TAKEAWAY

When you put a seed into the ground, it is not the plant that will grow, but only a dry little seed. God gives it a new body. God himself has prepared us for this.

Let us run with endurance the race that God has set before us. We do this by keeping our eyes on Jesus. . . . Think about all he endured when sinful people did such terrible things to him, so that you don't become weary and give up. After all, you have not yet given your lives in your struggle against sin. ❖ So take a new grip with your tired hands and stand firm on your shaky legs. ❖ The eyes of the Lord search the whole earth in order to strengthen those whose hearts are fully committed to him. (Hebrews 12:1-4, 12-13; 2 Chronicles 16:9)

Don't become weary and give up. We do this by keeping our eyes on Jesus.

MIND MENDER: I said to the man who stood at the gate of the year: Give me a light that I may tread safely into the unknown! And he replied: Go out into the darkness and put thine hand into the hand of God. That shall be to thee better than light and safer than a known way. —Unknown

Twelve

CONSOLATION

☐ 78 _____

The Lord is close to the brokenhearted; he rescues those who are crushed in spirit. The righteous face many troubles, but the Lord rescues them from each and every one. (Psalm 34:18-19)

TAKEAWAY
The righteous face many troubles, but the Lord rescues them from each and every one.

☐ 79 _____

The Lord is my rock, my fortress, and my savior; my God is my rock, in whom I find protection. He is my shield, the strength of my salvation, and my stronghold. I will call on the Lord, who is worthy of praise, for he saves me from my enemies. (Psalm 18:2-3)

He is my shield. I will call on the Lord for he saves me from my enemies.

□ 80 _____

O my people, trust in him at all times. Pour out your heart to him, for God is our refuge. (Psalm 62:8)

TAKEAWAY
Trust in him at all times.

□ 81 _____

No one can measure the depths of his understanding. ❖ [Lord,] you keep track of all my sorrows. You have collected all my tears in your bottle. You have recorded each one in your book. (Isaiah 40:28; Psalm 56:8)

TAKEAWAY
No one can measure the depths of his understanding.

□ 82 _____

I am holding you by your right hand—I, the Lord your God. And I say to you, "Do not be afraid. I am here to help you." (Isaiah 41:13)

TAKEAWAY
I am holding you by your right hand. Do not be afraid.

□ 83 _____

He gives power to those who are tired and worn
out; he offers strength to the weak. Even youths
will become exhausted, and young men will give
up. But those who wait on the Lord will find new
strength. They will fly high on wings like eagles.
They will run and not grow weary. They will walk
and not faint. (Isaiah 40:29-31)

TAKEAWAY

**Those who wait on the Lord will walk and not
faint.**

□ 84 _____

So don't worry about tomorrow, for tomorrow
will bring its own worries. Today's trouble is
enough for today. ❖ He has showered his kindness on us, along with all wisdom and understanding. (Matthew 6:34; Ephesians 1:8)

TAKEAWAY

**Don't worry about tomorrow, for tomorrow will
bring its own worries.**

MIND MENDER: Divine comfort does not come to us
in any mysterious or arbitrary way. The indwelling
Comforter "brings to remembrance" comforting things
concerning our Lord, and if we believe them, we are
comforted by them. A text is brought to our remembrance, perhaps, or the verse of a hymn, or some
thought concerning the love of Christ and his tender
care. If we receive the suggestion in simple faith, we
cannot help being comforted. But if we refuse to listen

to the voice of our Comforter, and insist instead on listening to the voice of discouragement or despair, no comfort can by any possibility reach our souls.
—Hannah W. Smith, *The God of All Comfort*

Thirteen

HOW TO BE UP IN A
DOWN WORLD

□ 85 _____

I am still not all I should be, but I am focusing all
my energies on this one thing: Forgetting the past
and looking forward to what lies ahead. ❖Let us
run with endurance the race that God has set
before us. We do this by keeping our eyes on
Jesus, on whom our faith depends from start to
finish. (Philippians 3:13; Hebrews 12:1-2)

TAKEAWAY
**Let us run with endurance the race that God has
set before us.**

_____

A relaxed attitude lengthens life. ❖Those who trust
the Lord will be happy. ❖Don't be impressed with
your own wisdom. Instead, fear the Lord and turn
your back on evil. Then you will gain renewed
health and vitality. (Proverbs 14:30; 16:20; 3:7-8)

T A K E A W A Y
**Those who trust the Lord will gain renewed
health and vitality.**

_____

Gentle words bring life and health; a deceitful
tongue crushes the spirit. ❖Why am I discouraged?
Why so sad? I will put my hope in God! ❖This is
the day the Lord has made. We will rejoice and be
glad in it. (Proverbs 15:4; Psalms 43:5; 118:24)

T A K E A W A Y
**This is the day the Lord has made. We will
rejoice and be glad in it.**

_____

Come unto me, all ye that labour and are heavy
laden, and I will give you rest. Take my yoke upon
you, and learn of me . . . and ye shall find rest
unto your souls. For my yoke is easy, and my burden is light. (Matthew 11:28-30, KJV)

T A K E A W A Y
**I will give you rest . . . for my yoke is easy, and
my burden is light.**

☐ 89 _____

Cast thy burden upon the Lord, and he shall sustain thee. ❖ Ye shall find rest for your souls. (Psalm 55:22; Jeremiah 6:16, KJV)

T A K E A W A Y
He shall sustain thee.

☐ 90 _____

Take no thought for your life, what ye shall eat, or what ye shall drink; nor yet for your body, what ye shall put on. Is not the life more than meat, and the body than raiment? ❖ Consider the lilies of the field, how they grow; they toil not, neither do they spin: and yet I say unto you, that even Solomon in all his glory was not arrayed like one of these. Wherefore, if God so clothe the grass of the field, which today is, and to morrow is cast into the oven, shall he not much more clothe you, O ye of little faith? ❖ Your heavenly Father knoweth that ye have need of all these things. (Matthew 6:25, 28-30, 32, KJV)

T A K E A W A Y
Your heavenly Father knows you have needs.

☐ 91 _____

Ye are of God, little children. Greater is he that is in you, than he that is in the world. ❖ In thee, O Lord, do I put my trust. (1 John 4:4; Psalm 71:1, KJV)

T A K E A W A Y
Ye are of God.

MIND MENDER:

> *Though waves and billows o'er me roll*
> *In crushing floods of ill,*
> *Within the haven of God's love*
> *My soul is anchored still.*
>
> —ANONYMOUS

Fourteen

LORD, I FEAR THAT I'M LOSING MY MIND

☐ 92 _____

God hath not given us the spirit of fear; but of power, and of love, and of a sound mind. ❖ Be not afraid of sudden fear . . . when it cometh. For the Lord shall be thy confidence, and shall keep thy foot from being taken. (2 Timothy 1:7; Proverbs 3:25-26, KJV)

TAKEAWAY
The Lord shall be thy confidence.

☐ 93 _____

The Lord also will be a refuge for the oppressed, a refuge in times of trouble. ❖ He will regard the prayer of the destitute, and not despise their prayer. (Psalms 9:9; 102:17, KJV)

He will regard the prayer of the destitute. He has not forsaken them that seek him.

☐ 94 _____

Be renewed in the spirit of your mind. ❖What time I am afraid, I will trust in thee. ❖There is no fear in love; but perfect love casteth out fear: because fear hath torment. He that feareth is not made perfect in love. (Ephesians 4:23; Psalm 56:3; 1 John 4:18, KJV)

TAKEAWAY
What time I am afraid, I will trust in thee.

☐ 95 _____

He that dwelleth in the secret place of the Most High shall abide under the shadow of the Almighty. I will say of the Lord, He is my refuge and my fortress: my God; in him I trust. ❖He shall cover thee with his feathers, and under his wings shalt thou trust; his truth shall be thy shield and buckler. Thou shalt not be afraid for the terror by night; nor for the arrow that flieth by day. (Psalm 91:1-2, 4-5, KJV)

TAKEAWAY
Thou shalt not be afraid. Under his wings shalt thou trust.

☐ 96 _____

Thou wilt keep him in perfect peace, whose mind is stayed on thee: because he trusteth in thee. ❖For he shall give his angels charge over thee, to keep thee in all thy ways. They shall bear thee up in their hands, lest thou dash thy foot against a stone. ❖ He hath set his love upon me. (Isaiah 26:3; Psalm 91:11-12, 14, KJV)

TAKEAWAY
He has set his love upon me.

☐ 97 _____

I hear the tumult of the raging seas as your waves and surging tides sweep over me. ❖ "O God my rock," I cry, "Why have you forsaken me?" ❖ Why am I discouraged? Why so sad? I will put my hope in God! I will praise him again—my Savior and my God! ❖ "Be silent, and know that I am God!" The Lord Almighty is here among us. (Psalms 42:7, 9, 11; 46:10-11)

TAKEAWAY
The Lord Almighty is here among us.

☐ 98 _____

Whatever things are true, whatever things are noble, whatever things are just, whatever things are pure, whatever things are lovely, whatever things are of good report. . . . If there is anything praiseworthy—meditate on these things. (Philippians 4:8, NKJV)

TAKEAWAY
"Whatever things are lovely, meditate on *these* things." In times of greatest mental stress, get

out a hymnbook, go to a quiet place, and read (better yet, sing!) the comforting words aloud.

MIND MENDER: O Lord, whose way is perfect, help us to always trust in your goodness, that walking with you and following you in all simplicity, we may possess quiet and contented minds; and may cast all our care on you, for you care about us. Please fill us with true worship and gratitude for all that you are for us, to us, and in us. Fill us with love, joy, peace, and all the fruits of the Spirit. Amen. —Christina G. Rossetti, adapted

Fifteen

PRACTICING THE PRESENCE OF GOD

☐ 99 _____

Because he is at my right hand, I will not be shaken. (Psalm 16:8, NIV)

TAKEAWAY
He is at my right hand.

☐ 100 _____

O Lord . . . you know me. You know when I sit and when I rise; you perceive my thoughts. . . . You discern my going out and my lying down; you are familiar with all my ways. ❖ You hem me in, behind and before. (Psalm 139:1-3, 5, NIV)

TAKEAWAY
You hem me in—behind and before.

☐ 101 _____

You, Lord, have never forsaken those who seek
you. (Psalm 9:10, NIV)

TAKEAWAY
**Lord, you have never forsaken those who seek
you.**

☐ 102 _____

Be sure of this: I am with you always, even to the
end of the age. ❖ The Lord your God is with you
wherever you go. (Matthew 28:20; Joshua 1:9)

TAKEAWAY
**Even to the end of the age, God is with you
wherever you go.**

☐ 103 _____

And I will ask the Father, and he will give you
another Counselor (or *Comforter*) who will never
leave you. He is the Holy Spirit. . . . I will not
abandon you as orphans—I will come to you.
(John 14:16-18)

TAKEAWAY
The Comforter will never leave you.

☐ 104 _____

This I declare of the Lord: He alone is my refuge,
my place of safety; he is my God, and I am trusting him. ❖ The Lord is close to all who call on

him . . . sincerely. ❖ He . . . never tires and never sleeps. (Psalms 91:2; 145:18; 121:4)

TAKEAWAY

He never tires and never sleeps. Brother Lawrence called prayer the "practice of the presence of God."

☐ 105 _____

I will make my people strong in my power, and they will go wherever they wish by my authority. I, the Lord, have spoken! (Zechariah 10:12)

TAKEAWAY

My people go wherever they wish by my authority.

MIND MENDER: I am alive. I am here. God is here with me. It is enough.

Sixteen

CENTERING MY MIND ON GOD'S INCREDIBLE POWER

☐ 106 _____

The earth is the Lord's, and everything in it. The world and all its people belong to him. For he laid the earth's foundation on the seas and built it on the ocean depths. ❖Who is the King of glory? The Lord Almighty—he is the King of glory. (Psalm 24:1-2, 10)

TAKEAWAY
He laid the earth's foundation on the seas and built it on the ocean depths.

☐ 107 _____

Prepare to meet your God. . . . For the Lord is the one who shaped the mountains, stirs up the winds, and reveals his every thought. He turns the light of dawn into darkness and treads the mountains under his feet. The Lord God Almighty is his name! ❖ Praise the Lord, I tell myself; O Lord my God, how great you are! (Amos 4:12-13; Psalm 104:1)

TAKEAWAY
The Lord is the one who shaped the mountains. O Lord my God, how great you are!

☐ 108 _____

You are robed with honor and with majesty; you are dressed in a robe of light. You stretch out the starry curtain of the heavens; you lay out the rafters of your home in the rain clouds. You make the clouds your chariots; you ride upon the wings of the wind. The winds are your messengers; flames of fire are your servants. You placed the world on its foundation so it would never be moved. (Psalm 104:1-5)

TAKEAWAY
You make the clouds your chariots; you ride upon the wings of the wind.

☐ 109 _____

Who else has held the oceans in his hand? Who has measured off the heavens with his fingers? Who else knows the weight of the earth or has weighed out the mountains and the hills? Who is able to advise the Spirit of the Lord? Who knows enough to be his teacher or counselor? Has the

Lord ever needed anyone's advice? . . . . No, for all the nations of the world are nothing in comparison with him. They are but a drop in the bucket, dust on the scales. He picks up the islands as though they had no weight at all. ❖ The nations of the world are as nothing to him. In his eyes they are less than nothing—mere emptiness and froth. (Isaiah 40:12-15, 17)

TAKEAWAY

Who is able to advise the Spirit of the Lord? Who knows enough to be his teacher or counselor? Has the Lord ever needed anyone's advice?

☐ 110 _____

[Christ] is the image of the invisible God, the first-born over all creation. For by him all things were created; things in heaven and on earth, visible and invisible, whether thrones or powers or rulers or authorities; all things were created by him and for him. He is before all things, and in him all things hold together. (Colossians 1:15-17, NIV)

TAKEAWAY

Christ is the image of the invisible God.

☐ 111 _____

To whom, then, can we compare God? What image might we find to resemble him? ❖ It is God who sits above the circle of the earth. . . . He is the one who spreads out the heavens like a curtain and makes his tent from them. He judges the great people of the world and brings them all to nothing. They hardly get started, barely taking root, when he blows on them and their work withers. The wind carries them off like straw. (Isaiah 40:18, 22-24)

TAKEAWAY

He blows on the great people of the world, and their work withers. The wind carries them off like straw.

□ 112 _____

I saw a throne in heaven and someone sitting on it! The one sitting on the throne was as brilliant as gemstones—jasper and carnelian. And the glow of an emerald circled his throne like a rainbow. . . . And from the throne came flashes of lightning and the rumble of thunder. . . . In front of the throne was a shiny sea of glass, sparkling like crystal. In the center and around the throne were four living beings. . . . Day after day and night after night they keep on saying, "Holy, holy, holy is the Lord God Almighty—the one who always was, who is, and who is still to come." (Revelation 4:2-8)

TAKEAWAY

The one sitting on the throne was as brilliant as gemstones, and the glow of an emerald circled his throne like a rainbow. Holy, holy, holy.

MIND MENDER: My troubles seem small when I remember how great my God is.

Seventeen

WHY SUFFERING,
LORD?

☐ 113 _____

"Return home, you wayward children." ❖ The
Lord still waits for you to come to him so he can
show you his love and compassion. For the Lord
is a faithful God. Blessed are those who wait for
him to help them. (Jeremiah 3:14; Isaiah 30:18)

TAKEAWAY
The Lord still waits for you to come to him so
he can show you his love and compassion.

☐ 114 _____

What I want . . . is your true thanks to God; I want
you to fulfill your vows to the Most High. Trust me
in your times of trouble, and I will rescue you, and

you will give me glory. ❖ Giving thanks is a sacrifice that truly honors me. (Psalm 50:14-15, 23)

Trust me in your times of trouble, and I will rescue you, and you will give me glory.

☐ 115 _____

As Jesus was walking along, he saw a man who had been blind from birth. "Teacher," his disciples asked him, "why was this man born blind? Was it a result of his own sins or those of his parents?" "It was not because of his sins or his parents' sins," Jesus answered. "He was born blind so the power of God could be seen in him. . . . Then he spit on the ground, made mud with the saliva, and smoothed the mud over the blind man's eyes. He told him, "Go and wash in the pool of Siloam." So the man went and washed, and came back seeing! ❖ Then the Pharisees once again questioned the man who had been blind and demanded, "This man who opened your eyes— who do you say he is?" The man replied, "I think he must be a prophet." ❖ "Yes, Lord," the man said, "I believe!" And he worshiped Jesus. (John 9:1-7, 17, 38)

TAKEAWAY
Jesus (suffering mental anguish because he knew his death on the cross was imminent) said, "Now my soul is deeply troubled. Should I pray, 'Father, save me from what lies ahead?' But

that is the very reason why I came! Father, bring glory and honor to your name." (John 12:27-28)

□ 116 _____

Wait on the Lord: be of good courage, and he shall strengthen thine heart: wait, I say, on the Lord. ❖That is why we never give up. Though our bodies are dying, our spirits are being renewed every day. (Psalm 27:14, KJV; 2 Corinthians 4:16)

TAKEAWAY
Our spirits are being renewed every day.

□ 117 _____

Even we Christians, although we have the Holy Spirit within us as a foretaste of future glory, also groan to be released from pain and suffering. . . . Now that we are saved, we eagerly look forward to this freedom. For if you already have something, you don't need to hope for it. But if we look forward to something we don't have yet, we must wait patiently and confidently. ❖All praise to the God and Father of our Lord Jesus Christ. He is the source of every mercy and the God who comforts us. He comforts us in all our troubles so that we can comfort others. When others are troubled, we will be able to give them the same comfort God has given us. You can be sure that the more we suffer for Christ, the more God will shower us with his comfort through Christ. Then you can patiently endure. (Romans 8:23-25; 2 Corinthians 1:3-6)

We groan to be released from pain and suffering. We look forward to something we don't have yet. We must wait patiently and confidently.

☐ 118 _____

Praise the Lord! Happy are those who fear the Lord. Yes, happy are those who delight in doing what he commands. ❖When darkness overtakes the godly, light will come bursting in. [The Lord] is generous, compassionate, and righteous. ❖Such people will not be overcome by evil circumstances. Those who are righteous will be long remembered. They do not fear bad news; they confidently trust the Lord to care for them. (Psalm 112:1, 4, 6-7)

TAKEAWAY
Bless the Lord, O my soul, and forget not all his benefits: who forgiveth all thine iniquities; who healeth all thy diseases. (Psalm 103:2-3, KJV)

☐ 119 _____

Love one another. ❖Bear one another's burdens. ❖[Always be] rejoicing in hope, patient in tribulation, continuing steadfastly in prayer. ❖ Rejoice with those who rejoice, and weep with those who weep. ❖Let us not grow weary in doing what is right, for we will reap at harvest time, if we do not give up. So then, whenever we have an opportunity, let us work for the good of all, and especially for those of the family of faith. (1 Thessalonians

4:9; Galatians 6:2, NRSV; Romans 12:12, 15, NKJV; Galatians 6:9-10, NRSV)

Just as our bodies have many parts and each part has a special function, so it is with Christ's body. We are all parts of his one body, and each of us has different work to do. And since we are all one body in Christ, we belong to each other, and each of us needs all the others. ❖ When others are happy, be happy with them. If they are sad, share their sorrow. (Romans 12:4-5, 15)

MIND MENDER: I took a terrible hit on the head. I was bedridden. I groaned. I begged God to take away the awful anxiety that resulted. My body shook incessantly, and I feared insanity. I wondered why God didn't hurry in bringing help. I spent hours praying, then trying (in my better moments) to conjure up places to go and new doctors to see so that I could get rid of the terrifying curse upon me. I wanted things to change—and quickly! But, the fact of the matter is that when I finally realized there was nothing—absolutely nothing—more that either I or the doctors could do to help, something *did* change: me! I was placed in the unfamiliar and uneasy (for me) situation of having to give up depending on my own human solutions and leave the outcome to God. When, in desperation, I figuratively grabbed hold of my heavenly Father's ankles and told him, "Lord, the battle is yours and I trust you," I became quite a different person, a different kind of Christian, a more trusting Christian, one who can now depend less on incessant planning and more easily leave the results of things to God. Too bad he had to lay me flat in bed to get "independent me" to stop trying to manipulate every situation and instead to trust him whatever the circumstances, whatever the outcome. Now I can say heartily, "Thanks, God."

Eighteen

FROM STRESS TO STRENGTH

☐ 120 _____

The Sovereign Lord is my strength! He will make me as surefooted as a deer and bring me safely over the mountains. (Habakkuk 3:19)

TAKEAWAY
The Lord is my strength. He will bring me safely over the mountains.

☐ 121 _____

In your strength I can crush an army; with my God I can scale any wall. As for God, his way is perfect. All the Lord's promises prove true. He is a shield for all who look to him for protection. (Psalm 18:29-30)

TAKEAWAY
In your strength I can scale any wall.

☐ 122 _____

For who is God except the Lord? Who but our God is a solid rock? God arms me with strength; he has made my way safe. He makes me as sure-footed as a deer, leading me safely along the mountain heights. (Psalm 18:31-33)

TAKEAWAY
He makes me as surefooted as a deer, leading me safely along the mountain heights.

☐ 123 _____

Have you never heard or understood? Don't you know that the Lord is the everlasting God, the Creator of all the earth? He never grows faint or weary. (Isaiah 40:28)

TAKEAWAY
God never grows faint or weary.

☐ 124 _____

The steps of the godly are directed by the Lord. ❖ [He has] made a wide path for my feet to keep them from slipping. ❖ The Lord lives! Blessed be my rock! May the God of my salvation be exalted! (Psalm 18:23, 36, 46)

TAKEAWAY
The steps of the godly are directed by the Lord.

But blessed are those who trust in the Lord and
have made the Lord their hope and confidence.
They are like trees planted along a riverbank, with
roots that reach deep into the water. Such trees are
not bothered by the heat or worried by long
months of drought. Their leaves stay green, and
they go right on producing delicious fruit.
(Jeremiah 17:7-8)

T A K E A W A Y
Blessed are those who trust in the Lord.

You will keep in perfect peace all who trust in you,
whose thoughts are fixed on you! Trust in the
Lord always, for the Lord God is the eternal Rock.
❖And we know that God causes everything to
work together for the good of those who love God
and are called according to his purpose for them.
(Isaiah 26:3-4; Romans 8:28)

T A K E A W A Y
**Trust in the Lord always; we know that God
causes everything to work together for the good
of those who love God.**

MIND MENDER: Dear God, our entire lives have been
journeys of mercies and blessings shown to those most
undeserving of them. Year after year you have carried
us on, removed dangers from our paths, refreshed us,
been patient with us, directed us, sustained us. O, don't
leave us when we are weak and faithless. We know you

will stay with us, that we can rest assured in you. As we are true to your ways, you will, to the very end, be superabundantly good to us. We may rest upon your arm; we can sleep like babies in their mothers' laps. Amen. —John Henry Newman, adapted

Nineteen

PRAYING THE PSALMS

☐ 127 _____

Give ear to my words, O Lord, consider my meditation. Hearken unto the voice of my cry, my King, and my God: for unto thee will I pray. My voice shalt thou hear in the morning, O Lord; in the morning will I direct my prayer unto thee, and will look up. ❖ Let all those that put their trust in thee rejoice: let them ever shout for joy, because thou defendest them: let them also that love thy name be joyful in thee. For thou, Lord, wilt bless the righteous; with favour wilt thou compass him as with a shield. (Psalm 5:1-3, 11-12, KJV)

TAKEAWAY
In the morning will I direct my prayer unto thee, and will look up.

□ 128 _____

O Lord our Lord, how excellent is thy name in all
the earth! who hast set thy glory above the heavens. ❖When I consider thy heavens, the work of
thy fingers, the moon and the stars, which thou
hast ordained; What is man, that thou art mindful
of him? and the son of man, that thou visitest
him? ❖O Lord, our Lord, how excellent is thy
name in all the earth! (Psalm 8:1, 3-4, 9, KJV)

TAKEAWAY
**O Lord, our Lord, how excellent is thy name in
all the earth!**

□ 129 _____

Lord, thou hast been our dwelling place in all generations. Before the mountains were brought
forth, or ever thou hadst formed the earth and the
world, even from everlasting to everlasting, thou
art God. ❖A thousand years in thy sight are but as
yesterday when it is past, and as a watch in the
night. ❖The days of our years are threescore years
and ten . . . yet is their strength labour and sorrow;
for it is cut off, and we fly away. ❖So teach us to
number our days, that we may apply our hearts
unto wisdom. ❖O satisfy us early with thy mercy;
that we may rejoice and be glad all our days. ❖Let
the beauty of the Lord our God be upon us: and
establish thou the work of our hands. (Psalm 90:1-
2, 4, 10, 12, 14, 17, KJV)

TAKEAWAY
Let the beauty of the Lord our God be upon us.

The Lord executeth righteousness and judgment for all that are oppressed. ❖The Lord is merciful and gracious, slow to anger, and plenteous in mercy. ❖As the heaven is high above the earth, so great is his mercy toward them that fear him. (Psalm 103:6, 8, 11, KJV)

TAKEAWAY

The Lord executeth righteousness and judgment for all that are oppressed.

The Lord is like a father to his children, tender and compassionate to those who fear him. For he understands how weak we are; he knows we are only dust. Our days on earth are like grass; like wildflowers, we bloom and die. The wind blows, and we are gone—as though we had never been here. But the love of the Lord remains forever with those who fear him. . . . The Lord has made the heavens his throne; from there he rules over everything. Praise the Lord, you angels of his, you mighty creatures who carry out his plans, listening for each of his commands. Yes, praise the Lord, you armies of angels who serve him and do his will! Praise the Lord, everything he has created, everywhere in his kingdom. (Psalm 103:13-22)

TAKEAWAY

Praise the Lord, everything he has created, everywhere in his kingdom.

O give thanks unto the Lord, for he is good: for
his mercy endureth for ever. ❖They that go
down to the sea in ships, that do business in
great waters; These see the works of the Lord,
and his wonders in the deep. For he com-
mandeth, and raiseth the stormy wind, which
lifteth up the waves thereof. ❖They cry unto the
Lord in their trouble. . . . He maketh the storm a
calm, so that the waves thereof are still. Then
they are glad because they be quiet; so he
bringeth them unto their desired haven. O that
men would praise the Lord for his . . . wonderful works to the children of men! (Psalm 107:1,
23-25, 28-31, KJV)

TAKEAWAY
He maketh the storm a calm.

☐ 133

Keep back thy servant also from presumptuous
sins; let them not have dominion over me. . . . Let
the words of my mouth, and the meditation of
my heart, be acceptable in thy sight, O Lord, my
strength, and my redeemer. (Psalm 19:13-14, KJV)

TAKEAWAY
Let the words of my mouth and the meditation
of my heart be acceptable in thy sight, Lord.

MIND MENDER: O Lord, support us all the day long,
until the shadows lengthen, and the evening comes,
and the busy world is hushed, and the fever of life is

over and our work is done. Then, in thy mercy, grant us a safe lodging, and a holy rest, and peace at the last. —*Book of Common Prayer*

Twenty

LORD, I CAN'T SLEEP

☐ 134 _____

I will lie down in peace and sleep, for you alone,
O Lord, will keep me safe. (Psalm 4:8)

TAKEAWAY
I will lie down in peace and sleep.

☐ 135 _____

Oh, the joys of those who do not follow the
advice of the wicked. . . . But they delight in doing
everything the Lord wants; day and night they
think about his law. ❖Don't sin by letting anger
gain control over you. Think about it overnight
and remain silent. Offer proper sacrifices, and
trust in the Lord. ❖God gives rest to his loved
ones. (Psalms 1:1-2; 4:4-5; 127:2)

**Don't sin by letting anger gain control over you.
Think about it overnight and remain silent.**

☐ 136 _____

Morning, noon, and night I plead aloud in my distress, and the Lord hears my voice. ❖As for me, I
am poor and needy, but the Lord is thinking
about me right now. You are my helper and my
savior. (Psalms 55:17; 40:17)

The Lord is thinking about me right now.

☐ 137 _____

I thank God for you. . . . Night and day I constantly
remember you in my prayers. (2 Timothy 1:3)

I constantly remember you in my prayers.

☐ 138 _____

Don't be ashamed to be as a child in your relation-
ship to God. Let the everlasting arms rock you to
sleep. In complete trust, relax on God's amazing
kindliness. He will take care of you day and night,
forever. —Dr. Norman Vincent Peale, "You Can
Relax" (pamphlet)

Let the everlasting arms rock you to sleep.

The day is thine, the night also is thine. ❖I will lift up mine eyes unto the hills, from whence cometh my help. My help cometh from the Lord, which made heaven and earth. He will not suffer thy foot to be moved: he that keepeth thee will not slumber. ❖The Lord is thy keeper: the Lord is thy shade upon thy right hand. The sun shall not smite thee by day, nor the moon by night. . . . The Lord shall preserve thy going out and thy coming in from this time forth, and even for evermore. (Psalms 74:16; 121:1-3, 5-8, KJV)

TAKEAWAY
He that keepeth thee will not slumber.

My soul shall be satisfied . . . when I remember thee upon my bed, and meditate on thee in the night watches. Because thou hast been my help, therefore in the shadow of thy wings will I rejoice. (Psalm 63:5-7, KJV)

TAKEAWAY
My Help, in the night, in the shadow of thy wings will I rejoice.

MIND MENDER:
> *Ere thou sleepest, gently lay*
> *Every troubled thought away;*
> *Put off worry and distress*
> *As thou puttest off thy dress;*
> *Drop thy burden and thy care*

In the quiet arms of prayer.
Lord thou knowest how I live,
All I've done amiss forgive;
All of good I've tried to do
Strengthen, bless and carry through;
All I love in safety keep
While in Thee I fall asleep.

—HENRY VAN DYKE

Twenty-One

HE KNOWS MY NAME

☐ 141 _____

The gatekeeper opens the gate. . . . The sheep hear
his voice and come to him. He calls his own
sheep by name and leads them out. After he has
gathered his own flock, he walks ahead of them,
and they follow him because they recognize his
voice. ❖ I am the good shepherd; I know my own
sheep, and they know me. (John 10:3-4, 14)

TAKEAWAY
He calls his own sheep by name.

☐ 142 _____

Before I formed thee in the belly I knew thee.
❖ He himself gives life and breath to everything.
(Jeremiah 1:5, KJV; Acts 17:25)

Before I formed thee in the belly, I knew thee.

☐ 143 _____

The Lord knows those who are his. ❖ He has identified us as his own by placing the Holy Spirit in
our hearts as the first installment of everything he
will give us. (2 Timothy 2:19; 2 Corinthians 1:22)

T A K E A W A Y
He has identified us as his own.

☐ 144 _____

I will make you [mine] forever, showing you
righteousness and justice, unfailing love and
compassion. ❖ He is a mighty savior. He will
rejoice over you with great gladness. (Hosea 2:19;
Zephaniah 3:17)

T A K E A W A Y
**I will make you mine forever, showing you love
and compassion.**

☐ 145 _____

You know when I sit down or stand up. You
know my every thought when far away. . . . Every
moment you know where I am. You know what
I am going to say even before I say it, Lord.
(Psalm 139:2-4)

T A K E A W A Y
Every moment you know where I am.

Are not five sparrows sold for two cents? And yet
not one of them is forgotten by God. Indeed, the
very hairs of your head are all numbered. Do not
fear; you are of more value than many sparrows.
(Luke 12:6-7, NASB)

TAKEAWAY

The very hairs on your head are all numbered.

I created you and have cared for you since before
you were born. I will be your God throughout
your lifetime. . . . I made you, and I will care for
you. ❖ Sing for joy, O heavens! Rejoice, O earth!
Burst into song, O mountains! . . . [They say,]
"The Lord has deserted us; the Lord has forgotten
us." Never! Can a mother forget her nursing
child? Can she feel no love for a child she has
borne? But even if that were possible, I would not
forget you! See, I have written your name on my
hand. (Isaiah 46:3-4; 49:13-16)

TAKEAWAY

**I made you, and I will care for you. I have writ-
ten your name on my hand.**

MIND MENDER: I am not just a computer number. My
heavenly Father who saw me and cared for me inside
my dear mother's womb still knows me intimately by
face, by name, by need, by deed.

Twenty-Two

YOU AND ME, LORD

☐ 148 _____

My voice shalt thou hear in the morning, O Lord;
in the morning will I direct my prayer unto thee,
and will look up. ❖Lead me, O Lord, in thy righteousness. ❖Thou, Lord, wilt bless the righteous;
with favour wilt thou compass him as with a
shield. (Psalm 5:3, 8, 12, KJV)

TAKEAWAY
**My voice shalt thou hear in the morning,
O Lord.**

☐ 149 _____

The Lord is my light and my salvation; whom
shall I fear? The Lord is the strength of my life; of
whom shall I be afraid? ❖One thing have I
desired of the Lord, that will I seek after; that I

may dwell in the house of the Lord all the days of
my life, to behold the beauty of the Lord, and to
inquire in his temple. For in the time of trouble
he shall hide me in his pavilion: in the secret of
his tabernacle shall he hide me; he shall set me
upon a rock. (Psalm 27:1, 4-5, KJV)

TAKEAWAY
**In the time of trouble he shall hide me in his
pavilion, in the secret place of his tabernacle.**

☐ 150 _____

Wait on the Lord: be of good courage, and he
shall strengthen thine heart. ❖ Blessed be the
Lord, because he hath heard the voice of my sup-
plications. The Lord is my strength and my shield;
my heart trusted in him, and I am helped: therefore my heart greatly rejoiceth; and with my song
will I praise him. (Psalms 27:14; 28:6-7, KJV)

TAKEAWAY
**The Lord is my strength and my shield; I am
helped.**

☐ 151 _____

The Lord is the portion of mine inheritance and of
my cup. . . . I have a goodly heritage. ❖ Because he
is at my right hand, I shall not be moved. ❖ Keep
me as the apple of the eye, hide me under the
shadow of thy wings. (Psalms 16:5-6, 8; 17:8, KJV)

TAKEAWAY
Lord, keep me as the apple of the eye.

☐ 152 _____

The Lord is my shepherd; I shall not want. He maketh me to lie down in green pastures: he leadeth me beside the still waters. He restoreth my soul: he leadeth me in the paths of righteousness for his name's sake. (Psalm 23:1-3, KJV)

TAKEAWAY
He leadeth me beside the still waters.

☐ 153 _____

In God I have put my trust. ❖ Who is this King of glory? The Lord strong and mighty, the Lord mighty in battle. . . . The Lord of hosts, he is the King of glory. ❖ Unto thee, O Lord, do I lift up my soul. ❖ Thou art the God of my salvation; on thee do I wait all the day. (Psalms 56:4; 24:8-10; 25:1, 5, KJV)

TAKEAWAY
Unto thee, O Lord, do I lift up my soul. On thee do I wait all the day.

☐ 154 _____

What man is he that feareth the Lord? . . . His soul shall dwell at ease; and his seed shall inherit the earth. ❖ Mine eyes are ever toward the Lord; for he shall pluck my feet out of the net. ❖ My foot standeth in an even place. (Psalms 25:12-13, 15; 26:12, KJV)

TAKEAWAY
My soul shall dwell at ease.

MIND MENDER:

He leadeth me, O blessed thought!
O words with heavenly comfort fraught!
Whate'er I do, where'er I be,
Still 'tis God's hand that leadeth me.

—JOSEPH GILMORE, *"He Leadeth Me"*

Twenty-Three

PRAYERS FOR
HURTING PEOPLE
TO PRAY

□ 155 _____

[Jesus] went to the mount of Olives . . . and
kneeled down, and prayed saying, Father, if thou
be willing, remove this cup from me: nevertheless
not my will, but thine, be done. And there
appeared an angel unto him from heaven,
strengthening him. (Luke 22:39-43, KJV)

TAKEAWAY
Not my will, but thine, be done.

□ 156 _____

O Lord, you alone can heal me; you alone can
save. My praises are for you alone! ❖ Lord, do not
desert me now! You alone are my hope in the day
of disaster. (Jeremiah 17:14, 17)

You alone are my hope.

□ 157 _____

For days I mourned, fasted, and prayed to the God of heaven. Then I said, "O Lord, God of heaven, the great and awesome God who keeps his covenant of unfailing love with those who love him and obey his commands, listen to my prayer! Look down and see me praying night and day. . . . We have sinned terribly by not obeying the commands, laws, and regulations that you gave us through your servant Moses." ❖ O Lord, please hear my prayer! Listen to the prayers of those of us who delight in honoring you. ❖ The God of heaven will help us succeed. (Nehemiah 1:4-7, 11; 2:20)

TAKEAWAY
The God of heaven will help us succeed.

□ 158 _____

O Lord God of our fathers, art not thou God in heaven? and rulest not thou over all the kingdoms of the heathen? and in thine hand is there not power and might, so that none is able to withstand thee? Art not thou our God? ❖ If, when evil cometh upon us, as the sword, judgment, or pestilence, or famine, we stand . . . in thy presence . . . and cry unto thee in our affliction, then thou wilt hear and help. ❖ Praise the Lord; for his mercy endureth for ever. (2 Chronicles 20:6-7, 9, 21, KJV)

When evil cometh upon us, thou wilt hear and help. Praise the Lord.

☐ 159 _____

Be not far from me; for trouble is near; for there is none to help. ❖I am poured out like water, and all my bones are out of joint: my heart is like wax; it is melted. . . . My strength is dried up. ❖Be not thou far from me, O Lord: O my strength, haste thee to help me. ❖I will declare thy name unto my brethren: in the midst of the congregation will I praise thee. . . . Praise him. . . . For he hath not despised nor abhorred the affliction of the afflicted; neither hath he hid his face from him; but when he cried unto him, he heard. (Psalm 22:11, 14-15, 19, 22-24, KJV)

TAKEAWAY
He hath not hid his face from the afflicted. O my Strength, haste thee to help me.

☐ 160 _____

Oh, how I praise the Lord. . . . For he took notice of his lowly servant girl, and now generation after generation will call me blessed. For he, the Mighty One, is holy, and he has done great things for me. His mercy goes on from generation to generation, to all who fear him. His mighty arm does tremendous things! How he scatters the proud and haughty ones! He has taken princes from their thrones and exalted the lowly. He has satisfied the hungry with good things and sent the rich away with empty hands. (Luke 1:46-53)

TAKEAWAY
His mighty arm does tremendous things!

☐ 161 _____

Our Father which art in heaven, hallowed be thy name. Thy kingdom come. Thy will be done in earth, as it is in heaven. Give us this day our daily bread. And forgive us our debts, as we forgive our debtors. And lead us not into temptation, but deliver us from evil: for thine is the kingdom, and the power, and the glory, for ever. Amen. (Matthew 6:9-13, KJV)

TAKEAWAY
Thy kingdom come.

MIND MENDER: The Lord will give strength unto his people. —Psalm 29:11, KJV

The Lord is the strength of my life. —Psalm 27:1, KJV

Ye shall receive power. —Acts 1:8, KJV

We are more than conquerors through him that loved us. —Romans 8:37, KJV

Be strong in the Lord, and in the power of his might. —Ephesians 6:10, KJV

Twenty-Four

PRAYING FOR
PEOPLE I LOVE

☐ 162 _____

The Lord bless thee, and keep thee: the Lord make
his face shine upon thee, and be gracious unto
thee: the Lord lift up his countenance upon thee,
and give thee peace. (Numbers 6:24-26, KJV)

TAKEAWAY
The Lord bless thee, and keep thee.

☐ 163 _____

God knows how much I love you. . . . I pray that
your love for each other will overflow more and
more, and that you will keep on growing in your
knowledge and understanding. For I want you to
understand what really matters, so that you may
live pure and blameless lives until Christ returns.

May you always be filled with the fruit of your salvation—those good things that are produced in
your life by Jesus Christ—for this will bring much
glory and praise to God. (Philippians 1:8-11)

T A K E A W A Y
**I pray that your love for each other will overflow
more and more, and that you will keep on growing in your knowledge and understanding.**

☐ 164 _____

So we have continued praying for you ever since
we first heard about you. We ask God to give you
a complete understanding of what he wants to do
in your lives, and we ask him to make you wise
with spiritual wisdom. Then the way you live will
always honor and please the Lord, and you will
continually do good, kind things for others. All
the while, you will learn to know God better and
better. We also pray that you will be strengthened
with his glorious power so that you will have all
the patience and endurance you need. May you be
filled with joy. (Colossians 1:9-11)

T A K E A W A Y
**We also pray that you will be strengthened with
his glorious power so that you will have all the
patience and endurance you need.**

☐ 165 _____

And so we keep on praying for you, that our God
will make you worthy of the life to which he called

you. And we pray that God, by his power, will fulfill
all your good intentions and faithful deeds. Then
everyone will give honor to the name of our Lord
Jesus because of you, and you will be honored
along with him. (2 Thessalonians 1:11-12)

TAKEAWAY

**We pray that our God will fulfill all your good
intentions and faithful deeds.**

☐ 166 _____

Night and day we pray earnestly for you, asking
God . . . to fill up anything that may still be missing in your faith. . . . May the Lord make your love
grow and overflow to each other and to everyone
else, just as our love overflows toward you. As a
result, Christ will make your hearts strong, blameless, and holy when you stand before God our
Father on that day when our Lord Jesus comes
with all those who belong to him. ❖ God has
called us to be holy, not to live impure lives.
(1 Thessalonians 3:10-13; 4:7)

TAKEAWAY

**We pray earnestly for you, asking God to fill up
anything that may still be missing in your faith.**

☐ 167 _____

May the Lord of peace himself always give you his
peace no matter what happens. The Lord be with
you all. ❖ May the God of peace . . . equip you
with all you need for doing his will. May he pro-

duce in you, through the power of Jesus Christ, all that is pleasing to him. (2 Thessalonians 3:16; Hebrews 13:20-21)

TAKEAWAY

As motivation to find time to pray regularly, say to yourself, "My prayers can cause God to influence the lives of people I care about, even those who will have nothing to do with him." Ask God to give you a fresh hunger and thirst for him and a strong desire to make intercession a regular part of your life. Then watch for ways in which he alters circumstances so that daily quiet times can be worked into your busy schedule. Don't forget to thank him when you see it happening.

☐ 168 _____

I'm not asking you to take them out of the world, but to keep them safe from the evil one. . . . Make them pure and holy by teaching them your words of truth. ❖ My Spirit will not leave them, and neither will these words I have given you. They will be on your lips and on the lips of your children and your children's children forever. (John 17:15-17; Isaiah 59:21)

TAKEAWAY

Make them pure and holy by teaching them your words of truth.

MIND MENDER: I bow before your holy Temple as I worship. I will give thanks to your name for your unfailing love and faithfulness, because your promises are backed by all the honor of your name. When I pray, you answer me; you encourage me by giving me the strength I need. —Psalm 138:2-3

Twenty-Five

I CAN'T RELAX

☐ 169 _____

Open my eyes to see the wonderful truths in your
law. ❖The words of the wise bring healing.
(Psalm 119:18; Proverbs 12:18)

TAKEAWAY
Since the words of the wise soothe and heal,
read Psalm 91 today. Memorize verses 11 and 12
to help you relax.

☐ 170 _____

Whatsoever things are true, whatsoever things are
honest, whatsoever things are just, whatsoever
things are pure, whatsoever things are lovely, whatsoever things are of good report, . . . think on

these things . . . and the God of peace shall be with you. (Philippians 4:8-9, KJV)

Whatsoever things are lovely, whatsoever things are good, think on these things.

☐ 171 _____

Don't copy the behavior and customs of this world, but let God transform you into a new person by changing the way you think. ❖ Fix your thoughts on what is true and honorable and right. Think about things that are pure and lovely and admirable. Think about things that are excellent and worthy of praise. (Romans 12:2; Philippians 4:8)

Let God transform you into a new person by changing the way you think. Think about things that are excellent and worthy of praise.

☐ 172 _____

Scripture tells us, "Be ye transformed by the renewing of your mind"(Romans 12:2). Concentrating on these verses will help transform your mind to a quieter mood: ❖ He will feed his flock like a shepherd. He will carry the lambs in his arms. (Isaiah 40:11) ❖ Though he slay me, yet will I trust in him. (Job 13:15, KJV)

Why worry? Are tomorrow's skies more blue
If on our beds we restless roll and toss,
With burning, sleepless eyes until the morn,
Just building bridges we may never cross?

—ANONYMOUS

☐ 173 _____

At midnight I rise to thank you. ❖O Lord, the
earth is full of your unfailing love. . . . You have
done many good things for me, Lord, just as you
promised. ❖You are good and do only good. ❖I
have put my hope in your word. ❖I will quietly
keep my mind on your decrees. (Psalm 119:62,
64-65, 68, 81, 95)

TAKEAWAY
I will quietly keep my mind on your decrees.

☐ 174 _____

When peace, like a river, attendeth my way,
When sorrows like sea billows roll
Whatever my lot, Thou has taught me to say,
It is well, it is well with my soul.

—HORATIO G. SPAFFORD, "It Is Well with My Soul"

TAKEAWAY
Whatever my lot, it is well with my soul.

☐ 175 _____

This I know: God is on my side. ❖Have mercy on
me, O God! . . . I look to you for protection. I will

hide beneath the shadow of your wings until this violent storm is past. ❖He will send help from heaven to save me, rescuing me from those who are out to get me. ❖For your unfailing love is as high as the heavens. Your faithfulness reaches to the clouds. (Psalms 56:9; 57:1, 3, 10)

T A K E A W A Y

I will hide beneath the shadow of your wings until this violent storm is past.

MIND MENDER: My friend Steve says he used to get somewhat discouraged by statistics showing that the average person's mind stays focused only eleven seconds before drifting. Often the new focus is worry about personal problems. Steve's tip to turn that negative fact to positive advantage is: Whenever your mind wanders, let the first stop be God. If you purposely drift to a subject like God's great power to work wonders in people's lives (Ephesians 3:20) or his mercy and love, or the fine, good things in others (Philippians 4:8), your mind will slow down. God's peace will flood your heart. The mind is purposely turned to a positive, uplifting subject, sometimes as often as every eleven seconds, and worry is forced out. Positive and negative cannot occupy the same space at the same time.

I like Steve's tip. It helps me experience God's continuing positiveness off and on all day to produce little spurts of relaxation here and there.

Twenty-Six

I FEEL SO HELPLESS

☐ 176 _____

God has said, "I will never fail you. I will never forsake you." That is why we can say with confidence, "The Lord is my helper, so I will not be afraid. What can mere mortals do to me?" (Hebrews 13:5-6)

TAKEAWAY
The Lord is my helper.

☐ 177 _____

It is not by force nor by strength, but by my Spirit, says the Lord Almighty. (Zechariah 4:6)

TAKEAWAY
You will succeed not by force but by my Spirit.

☐ 178 _____

There is no one like the God of Israel. He rides
across the heavens to help you, across the skies in
majestic splendor. The eternal God is your refuge,
and his everlasting arms are under you. (Deuteronomy 33:26-27)

T A K E A W A Y
**The eternal God is your refuge, and his everlast-
ing arms are under you.**

☐ 179 _____

For nothing is impossible with God. (Luke 1:37)

T A K E A W A Y
Nothing is impossible with God.

☐ 180 _____

He is a shield for all who take refuge in him.
❖ [He] is able to do immeasurably more than all
we ask or imagine, according to his power that
is at work within us. (Psalm 18:30; Ephesians
3:20, NIV)

T A K E A W A Y
**He is able to do far more than we would ever
dare to ask.**

☐ 181 _____

Insert your name in the blank spaces; then read
the sentences aloud, emphasizing the words as
indicated.

He will do it FOR you,_____
He will DO it for you, _____
HE will do it for you, _____
He WILL do it for you, _____

—ANNABEL GILLHAM, "Victorious Christian Life" seminar

TAKEAWAY

Not by my power; not by my might. HE will do it for me.

□ 182 _____

The Lord is king! He is robed in majesty. Indeed, the Lord is robed in majesty and armed with strength. The world is firmly established; it cannot be shaken. ❖Your throne, O Lord, has been established from time immemorial. You yourself are from the everlasting past. The mighty oceans have roared, O Lord. ❖The mighty oceans roar like thunder; the mighty oceans roar as they pound the shore. But mightier than the violent raging of the seas, mightier than the breakers on the shore—the Lord above is mightier than these! Your royal decrees cannot be changed. The nature of your reign, O Lord, is holiness forever. (Psalm 93:1-5)

TAKEAWAY

The Lord is robed in majesty and armed with strength.

MIND MENDER: Is anything too hard for the Lord?
—Genesis 18:14, KJV

Twenty-Seven

I FEEL SO ALONE

☐ 183 _____

The Lord rewarded me for doing right, because of
the innocence of my hands in his sight. (Psalm
18:24)

TAKEAWAY
**The Lord your God is with you wherever you go.
(Joshua 1:9)**

☐ 184 _____

I can never escape from your spirit! I can never get
away from your presence! If I go up to heaven,
you are there; if I go down to the place of the
dead, you are there. If I ride the wings of the morning, if I dwell by the farthest oceans, even there
your hand will guide me, and your strength will

support me. I could ask the darkness to hide me and the light around me to become night—but even in darkness I cannot hide from you. To you the night shines as bright as day. Darkness and light are both alike to you. (Psalm 139:7-12)

TAKEAWAY

I can never escape from your spirit! If I ride the wings of the morning, your hand will guide me.

☐ 185 _____

I am like an owl in the desert, like a lonely owl in a far-off wilderness. I lie awake, lonely as a solitary bird on the roof. ❖ He will listen to the prayers of the destitute. He will not reject their pleas. ❖ The Lord watches over those who fear him, those who rely on his unfailing love. (Psalms 102:6-7, 17; 33:18)

TAKEAWAY

Someone has said that an infant in its mother's womb feels the rhythm of her steps and is comforted by the beating of her warm heart for nine months. God knows the rhythm of my walking and my heart thoughts, too. He is as close as breathing.

☐ 186 _____

The steps of the godly are directed by the Lord. .... The Lord holds them by the hand. Once I was young, and now I am old. Yet I have never seen the godly forsaken, nor seen their children begging for bread. ❖ He will never abandon the godly. He will keep them safe forever. (Psalm 37:23-25, 28)

TAKEAWAY
He will never abandon the godly.

☐ 187 _____

I cannot flee His presence. Go where I will, He leads me, and watches me, and cares for me. The same Being who is now at work in the remotest domains of nature and of providence is also at my hand to make more full every moment of my being. When I walk by the wayside, He is along with me. When I enter into company amid all my forgetfulness of Him, He never forgets me. In the silent watches of the night, when my eyelids are closed and my spirit has sunk into unconsciousness, the observant eye of Him who never slumbers is upon me. —Thomas Chalmers

TAKEAWAY
When I walk by the wayside, he is along with me.

☐ 188 _____

Though you once were far away from God, now you have been brought near to him because of the blood of Christ. ❖ So now you . . . are no longer strangers and foreigners. You are citizens along with all of God's holy people. You are members of God's family. (Ephesians 2:13, 19)

You are no longer strangers. You are members of God's family.

☐ 189 _____

Because of Christ and our faith in him, we can now come fearlessly into God's presence, assured of his glad welcome. ❖ By [Christ] God reconciled everything to himself. He made peace with everything in heaven and on earth by means of his blood on the cross. (Ephesians 3:12; Colossians 1:20)

TAKEAWAY
Have you ever thought what it means to be able to summon at will the God of the world? Even with a privileged visitor to an earthly king, there is the palace antechamber, and the time must be at the pleasure of the king. But God's subjects can summon him to bedside, to workshop, and he is there. Your nearest earthly friend cannot be with you on the instant. Your Lord, your master, your divine Friend—yes! —Unknown

MIND MENDER: The Good Shepherd does not lose track of his sheep.

Twenty-Eight

I HAVE TOO MUCH TO DO!

☐ 190 _____

He leadeth me beside still waters. He restoreth my soul. ❖ God is our refuge and strength, a very present help in trouble. ❖ Be still, and know that I am God. (Psalms 23:2-3; 46:1, 10, KJV)

TAKEAWAY

Be still, and know that I am God.

☐ 191 _____

I lay My Loving Hands on you in blessing. Wait in love and longing to feel their tender pressure and, as you wait, courage and hope will flow into your being, irradiating all your lives with the warm sun of My Presence. ❖ Let all go. Loosen your hold on earth, its care, its worries, even its joys. Unclasp

your hands, relax and the tide of joy will come.
— *God Calling,* edited by A. J. Russell

Thou anointeth my head with oil. (Psalm 23:5, KJV)

☐ 192 _____

The race is not to the swift or the battle to the
strong. . . . No man knows when his hour will
come. ❖Whoever loves money never has money
enough; whoever loves wealth is never satisfied
with his income. (Ecclesiastes 9:11-12; 5:10, NIV)

T A K E A W A Y
**The race is not to the swift or the battle to the
strong.**

☐ 193 _____

There is a time for everything, and a season for
every activity: . . . a time to be born and a time to
die, a time to plant and a time to uproot, . . . a
time to tear down and a time to build, . . . a time
to mourn and a time to dance, . . . a time to
embrace and a time to refrain, a time to search
and a time to give up, . . . a time to be silent and a
time to speak, . . . a time for war and a time for
peace. ❖[God] has made everything beautiful in
its time. ❖That everyone may eat and drink, and
find satisfaction in all his toil—this is the gift of
God. (Ecclesiastes 3:1-8, 11, 13, NIV)

T A K E A W A Y
Everything . . . in its time.

Hidden in the hollow of His blessed hand,
Never foe can follow, never traitor stand;
Not a surge of worry, not a shade of care,
Not a blast of hurry touch the spirit there.

—FRANCES R. HAVERGAL, *"Like a River Glorious"*

TAKEAWAY
My best is good enough for today.

☐ 195

When I am jostled about on the crowded and noisy Peachtree Street bus at 5 o'clock in the afternoon—His banner over me is love. ❖When I am huddled with others sharing information with graphs and computers in a busy office conference high atop a downtown office building—His banner over me is love. ❖In a lonesome hospital bed, during the long, long uncertain night before my surgery—His banner over me was love. ❖When my kids talk back or when I am worried sick because someone I love is so ill—His banner over me is love. ❖When my spouse and I have a heated argument and we forget our love, then yell at each other—His banner over me is love. ❖When I begin to doubt my faith—His banner over me is love. ❖Blessed is the Lord for he has shown me that his never-failing love protects me like the walls of a fort (Psalm 31:21). —Busy Atlanta businesswoman-wife-mother

TAKEAWAY
His banner over me is love.

God gives good gifts. In this crazy, hyperactive world I say that I can't get enough rest. But Sunday was his idea.

TAKEAWAY

Remember the Sabbath day by keeping it holy. Six days you shall labor and do all your work, but the seventh day is a Sabbath to the Lord your God. . . . In six days the Lord made the heavens and the earth, the sea, and all that is in them, but he rested on the seventh day. (Exodus 20:8-11, NIV)

MIND MENDER: Practice lifting your mind above the confusion and irritation around you. Form mental pictures of the great hills or mountain ranges, or the wide sweep of the ocean, or of some great valley spreading out before you. Get a mental picture of the stars serene in the heavens, or of the moon sailing high on a clear, calm night. Hang these pictures on the walls of your mind and think about them habitually. One can do this while busy on the job. —Dr. Norman Vincent Peale, *A Guide to Confident Living*

Twenty-Nine

LOOK WHAT HAPPENED WHEN OTHERS PRAYED!

☐ 197 _____

When Isaac was forty years old, he married Rebekah. . . . Isaac pleaded with the Lord to give Rebekah a child because she was childless. So the Lord answered Isaac's prayer. (Genesis 25:20-21)

TAKEAWAY
When I pray, I will not dwell on the problem, but rather on the extraordinary capability of the great Problem Solver. "All authority in heaven and on earth has been given to me." (Matthew 28:18, NIV)

They took away the stone from the place where
the dead [Lazarus] was laid. And Jesus lifted up
his eyes, and said, Father, I thank thee that thou
hast heard me. . . . And when he thus had spoken,
he cried with a loud voice, Lazarus, come forth.
And he that was dead came forth, bound hand
and foot with graveclothes. (John 11:41-44, KJV)

TAKEAWAY
Lazarus came forth from the dead.

Near the shore where we landed was an estate
belonging to Publius, the chief official of the
island. . . . Publius's father was ill with fever and
dysentery. Paul went in and prayed for him, and
laying his hands on him, he healed him. Then all
the other sick people on the island came and were
cured. (Acts 28:7-9)

TAKEAWAY
**Paul went in and prayed for him, and laying his
hands on him, he healed him.**

They caught Paul and Silas . . . and brought them
to the magistrates. And the multitude rose up
together against them. . . and when they had laid
many stripes upon them, they cast them into
prison, charging the jailer to keep them safely:
who, having received such a charge, thrust them

into the inner prison, and made their feet fast in the stocks. And at midnight Paul and Silas prayed, and sang praises unto God: and the prisoners heard them.And suddenly there was a great earthquake, so that the foundations of the prison were shaken: and immediately all the doors were opened, and every one's bands were loosed. (Acts 16:19-27, KJV)

TAKEAWAY

In prison, Paul and Silas prayed, and sang praises. And suddenly the foundations of the prison were shaken and all the doors were opened.

☐ 201 _____

Elijah took twelve stones . . . to rebuild the Lord's altar. . . . He piled wood on the altar, cut the bull into pieces, and laid the pieces on the wood. Then he said, "Fill four large jars with water, and pour the water over the offering and the wood." ❖Elijah the prophet walked up to the altar and prayed, "O Lord, . . . prove today that you are God in Israel and that I am your servant. . . . O Lord, answer me! Answer me so these people will know that you, O Lord, are God and that you have brought them back to yourself." Immediately the fire of the Lord flashed down from heaven and burned up the young bull, the wood, the stones, and the dust. It even licked up all the water in the ditch! And when the people saw it, they fell on their faces and cried out, "The Lord is God! The Lord is God!" (1 Kings 18:31-33, 36-39)

I will call on God, and the Lord will rescue me.
❖ He rescues me and keeps me safe from the
battle waged against me, even though many still
oppose me. ❖ He will send help from heaven to
save me, rescuing me from those who are out to
get me. (Psalm 55:16, 18; 57:3)

☐ 202 _____

When Elisha arrived, the child was indeed dead.
He went in alone and shut the door behind him
and prayed to the Lord. Then he lay down on the
child's body, placing his mouth on the child's
mouth, his eyes on the child's eyes, and his hands
on the child's hands. And the child's body began
to grow warm again! . . . The boy sneezed seven
times and opened his eyes! (2 Kings 4:32-35)

TAKEAWAY
I will answer them before they even call to me.
While they are still talking to me about their
needs, I will go ahead and answer their prayers!
(Isaiah 65:24)

☐ 203 _____

So Joshua and the entire Israelite army left Gilgal
and set out to rescue Gibeon. ❖ Joshua traveled
all night from Gilgal and took the Amorite armies
by surprise. The Lord threw them into a panic,
and the Israelites slaughtered them in great numbers at Gibeon. ❖ On the day the Lord gave the
Israelites victory over the Amorites, Joshua prayed

to the Lord in front of all the people of Israel. He said, "Let the sun stand still over Gibeon, and the moon over the valley of Aijalon." So the sun and moon stood still until the Israelites had defeated their enemies. The sun stopped in the middle of the sky, and it did not set as on a normal day. Never before or since has there been a day like that one, when the Lord answered such a request from a human being. (Joshua 10:7, 9-10, 12-14)

TAKEAWAY
The sun stopped in the middle of the sky, and it did not set as on a normal day. Never before or since has there been a day when the Lord answered such a request from a human being.

MIND MENDER: Think upon me, my God, for good. —Nehemiah 5:19, KJV

Thirty

LOOK WHAT HAPPENED WHEN OTHERS PRAYED! (cont.)

☐ 204 _____

Samson called unto the Lord, and said, O Lord God, remember me, I pray thee, and strengthen me, I pray thee, only this once, O God, that I may be at once avenged of the Philistines for my two eyes. And Samson took hold of the two middle pillars upon which the house stood, and on which it was borne up, of the one with his right hand, and of the other with his left. And Samson said, Let me die with the Philistines. And he bowed himself with all his might; and the house fell upon the lords, and upon all the people that were therein. So the dead which he slew at his death were more than they which he slew in his life. (Judges 16:28-30, KJV)

**I am the Lord, the God of all mankind. Is any-
thing too hard for me? (Jeremiah 32:27, NIV)**

□ 205 _____

So the Lord told Abraham, "I have heard that the
people of Sodom and Gomorrah are extremely
evil, and that everything they do is wicked."
❖Abraham approached him and said, "Will you
destroy both innocent and guilty alike? Suppose
you find fifty innocent people there within the
city—will you still destroy it, and not spare it for
their sakes? . . . Suppose there are only forty? . . .
thirty? . . . twenty? . . . ten?" And the Lord said,
"Then, for the sake of the ten, I will not destroy
it." The Lord went on his way when he had fin-
ished his conversation with Abraham. (Genesis
18:20, 23-33)

> *More things are wrought by prayer*
> *Than this world dreams of.*
> *Wherefore, let thy voice*
> *Rise like a fountain for me night and day.*
>
> —ALFRED, LORD TENNYSON, *"Idylls of the King"*

□ 206 _____

When Hezekiah realized that Sennacherib also
intended to attack Jerusalem, he consulted with
his officials and military advisers. ❖ "Be strong
and courageous! Don't be afraid of the king of
Assyria or his mighty army, for there is a power far

greater on our side! . . . We have the Lord our God to help us and to fight our battles for us!" ❖Then King Hezekiah and the prophet Isaiah son of Amoz cried out in prayer to God in heaven. And the Lord sent an angel who destroyed the Assyrian army with all its commanders and officers. (2 Chronicles 32:2-3, 7-8, 20-21)

T A K E A W A Y

Hezekiah and Isaiah cried out in prayer to God, and the Lord sent an angel.

☐ 207 _____

Teach me how to live, O Lord. Lead me along the path of honesty, for my enemies are waiting for me to fall. Do not let me fall into their hands. ❖O Lord, you are my rock of safety. Please help me; don't refuse to answer me. Listen to my prayer for mercy as I cry out to you for help. . . . Don't drag me away with the wicked. . . . Give them the punishment they so richly deserve! ❖Praise the Lord! For he has heard my cry for mercy. . . . I trust in him with all my heart. He helps me, and my heart is filled with joy. I burst out in songs of thanksgiving. The Lord protects his people and gives victory to his anointed king. (Psalms 27:11-12; 28:1-4, 6-8)

T A K E A W A Y

Praise the Lord! For he has heard my cry for mercy. I trust in him with all my heart and he helps me.

For five years, I prayed for a beloved cousin that he might find the Lord in his life. It wasn't happening. I nearly gave up hope many times. Then another five years went by, and I prayed over and over and over. Then, another. I kept praying and believing, sometimes without much hope, just because I loved him and I knew the Lord was able. ❖Then came the letter . . . twenty years later! This much-loved man that I had grown up with was telling me that he and his wife were serving the Lord, whom they had recently found, in a strong church along with their children! When it happened, I was stunned. There were tears of joy. ❖ Now, my eyes are ever looking with new courage and perseverance to the Lord for other help because he heard my cries in the past. Who is this Lord? He is strong and mighty, the invincible commander of all of heaven's armies! He is able to do infinitely beyond whatever I ask or dream.

TAKEAWAY

The Lord receives my prayer. ❖ O Lord, Thou hast heard the desire of the humble; Thou wilt strengthen their heart, Thou wilt incline Thine ear. (Psalm 6:9; 10:17, NASB)

The Lord will not reject his people; he will not abandon his own special possession. ❖Unless the Lord had helped me, I would soon have died. I cried out, "I'm slipping!" and your unfailing love, O Lord, supported me. ❖You thrill me, Lord, with all you have done for me! . . . O Lord, what great miracles you do! And how deep are your thoughts. Only an ignorant person would not know this! ❖You are exalted in the heavens. You, O Lord, continue forever. (Psalms 94:14, 17-18; 92:4-6, 8)

TAKEAWAY
I cried out, "I'm slipping!" and your unfailing love, O Lord, supported me.

☐ 210 _____

From Daniel 6: ❖The other administrators and princes began searching for some fault in the way Daniel was handling his affairs, but they couldn't find anything to criticize. So they concluded, "Our only chance of finding grounds for accusing Daniel will be in connection with the requirements of his religion." ❖So the administrators and princes went to the king and said, "[We] have unanimously agreed that Your Majesty should make a law that will be strictly enforced. Give orders that for the next thirty days anyone who prays to anyone, divine or human—except to Your Majesty— will be thrown to the lions. And let Your Majesty issue and sign this law so it cannot be changed." Darius signed the law. ❖But when Daniel learned that the law had been signed, he went home and knelt down as usual in his upstairs room. He prayed three times a day, just as he had always done, giving thanks to his God. The officials found him praying. So they went back to the king

and reminded him about his law. ❖ The king was very angry with himself for signing the law, and he tried to find a way to save Daniel. He spent the rest of the day looking for a way to get Daniel out of this predicament. At last the king gave orders for Daniel to be arrested and thrown into the den of lions. The king said to him, "May your God, whom you worship continually, rescue you."
❖ Very early the next morning, the king hurried out to the lions' den. He called out in anguish, "Daniel, servant of the living God! Was your God, whom you worship continually, able to rescue you from the lions?" ❖ Daniel answered, "Long live the king! My God sent his angel to shut the lions' mouths so that they would not hurt me, for I have been found innocent in his sight. And I have not wronged you, Your Majesty." ❖ The king was overjoyed and ordered that Daniel be lifted from the den. Then King Darius sent this message to the people of every race and nation and language throughout the world:

TAKEAWAY

[Daniel's God] is the living God, and he will endure forever. His kingdom will never be destroyed, and his rule will never end. He rescues and saves his people; he performs miraculous signs and wonders in the heavens and on earth. (Daniel 6:26-27)

MIND MENDER: Well does the hymn put it: "Thou art coming to a King: Large petitions with thee bring." We do not come to the back door of the house of mercy to receive the broken scraps . . . nor to eat the crumbs

that fall from the Master's table. But when we pray, we are standing in the palace, on the glittering floor of the great King's own reception room. We stand where angels bow with veiled faces, where the cherubim and seraphim adore. Shall we come there with stunted requests, and narrow and contracted faith? He distributes gold! Do not bring before God stinted petitions and narrow desires. Remember, as high as the heavens are above the earth, so high are His ways above your ways, and His thoughts above your thoughts. Ask for great things, for you are before a great throne of grace.
—Charles H. Spurgeon

Thirty-One

ARE YOU LISTENING, LORD?

☐ 211 _____

The Holy Spirit helps us in our distress. For we don't even know what we should pray for, nor how we should pray. But the Holy Spirit prays for us with groanings that cannot be expressed in words. And the Father who knows all hearts knows what the Spirit is saying, for the Spirit pleads for us believers in harmony with God's own will. (Romans 8:26-27)

TAKEAWAY
The Holy Spirit prays for us with groanings that cannot be expressed in words.

☐ 212 _____

Keep on praying. ❖ Pray at all times and on every occasion in the power of the Holy Spirit. Stay alert and be persistent in your prayers for all Christians everywhere. (1 Thessalonians 5:17; Ephesians 6:18)

TAKEAWAY
Pray at all times and on every occasion.

☐ 213 _____

He will listen to the prayers of the destitute. He will not reject their pleas. (Psalm 102:17)

TAKEAWAY
He will listen; he is never too busy. When the enemy suggests many things for me to do early in the morning, I reply, "Excuse me, He is waiting." —Cameron V. Thompson, *Master Secrets of Prayer* (booklet)

☐ 214 _____

Christ has entered into heaven itself to appear now before God as our Advocate. ❖ Our High Priest sat down in the place of highest honor in heaven, at God's right hand. (Hebrews 9:24; 8:1)

TAKEAWAY
Christ has entered heaven to appear before God as my friend.

☐ 215 _____

If I could hear Christ praying for me in the next room, I would not fear a million enemies. Yet distance makes no difference. He *is* praying for me! —Robert M. McCheyne

For a few months, keep a prayer notebook and record God's answers. His "yeses" will both surprise and encourage. Rejoice, too, at the times God was right in *not* letting you have your own way.

☐ 216 _____

The Lord is far from the wicked but he hears the prayer of the righteous. ❖ "For I know the plans I have for you," says the Lord. "They are plans for good and not for disaster, to give you a future and a hope. In those days when you pray, I will listen. If you look for me in earnest, you will find me when you seek me." (Proverbs 15:29, NIV; Jeremiah 29:11-13)

TAKEAWAY
"When you pray, I will listen," says the Lord.

☐ 217 _____

If you feel inadequate coming to God as a newer or somewhat weaker or less knowledgeable Christian, or because you know your own imperfect heart so well, apply Hannah W. Smith's motto for confidence: "Green apples are apples too!" ❖ Envision yourself as his beloved child, skipping happily toward the heavenly prayer throne with bold confidence because he has adopted you into his family. Picture your Father welcoming you with open arms and a broad smile. Confess any sin in your life, then say, "I'm clean, I'm clean, praise

God I'm clean through the blood of Christ." Then say, "Of course my Father hears his good, clean, forgiven child. The path is clear between us."

TAKEAWAY
His unchanging plan has always been to adopt us into his own family by bringing us to himself through Jesus Christ. And this gave him great pleasure. (Ephesians 1:5)

MIND MENDER: I love the Lord because he hears and answers my prayers. Because he bends down and listens, I will pray as long as I have breath!
—Psalm 116:1-2

Thirty-Two

ANGELS HELPING

☐ 218 _____

God calls his angels "messengers swift as the wind, and servants made of flaming fire." ❖ Angels are only servants. They are spirits sent from God to care for those who will receive salvation. (Hebrews 1:7, 14)

TAKEAWAY

Angels are spirits sent from God to care for those who will receive salvation.

☐ 219 _____

For he orders his angels to protect you wherever you go. They will hold you with their hands to keep you from striking your foot on a stone. ❖The Lord says, "I will rescue those who love me. I will

133

protect those who trust in my name." (Psalm 91:11-12, 14)

TAKEAWAY

His angels will hold you with their hands to keep you from striking your foot on a stone.

☐ 220 _____

There was a certain beggar named Lazarus . . . full of sores, and desiring to be fed with the crumbs which fell from the rich man's table: moreover the dogs came and licked his sores. And it came to pass, that the beggar died, and was carried by the angels into Abraham's bosom. (Luke 16:20-22, KJV)

TAKEAWAY

Whether angel stories appear in the Bible or in conversation with a friend next door, one of the first and most elemental things we learn about the work of angels is that they *help* people. Caring for human beings ranks high on their list of duties. —Timothy Jones, *Celebration of Angels*

☐ 221 _____

I will extol the Lord at all times. . . . My soul will boast in the Lord. ❖Those who look to him are radiant. ❖The angel of the Lord encamps around those who fear him, and he delivers them. ❖Taste and see that the Lord is good; blessed is the man who takes refuge in him. ❖The eyes of the Lord are on the righteous and his ears are attentive to their cry. (Psalm 34:1-2, 5, 7, 8, 15, NIV)

TAKEAWAY
The angel of the Lord encamps around those who fear him.

□ 222 _____

Jesus was led by the Spirit into the desert to be tempted by the devil. After fasting forty days and forty nights, he was hungry. ❖The devil took him to the holy city and had him stand on the highest point of the temple. "If you are the Son of God," he said, "throw yourself down. For it is written: 'He will command his angels concerning you, and they will lift you up in their hands, so that you will not strike your foot against a stone.'" ❖Again, the devil took him to a very high mountain and showed him all the kingdoms of the world and their splendor. "All this I will give you," he said, "if you will bow down and worship me." Jesus said to him, "Away from me, Satan!" . . . Then the devil left him, and angels came and attended him. (Matthew 4:1-2, 5-6, 8-11, NIV)

TAKEAWAY
Angels came and attended him.

□ 223 _____

Peter was kept in prison, but the church was earnestly praying to God for him. . . . Peter was sleeping between two soldiers, bound with two chains, and sentries stood guard at the entrance. Suddenly an angel of the Lord appeared and a light shone in the cell. He struck Peter on the side and woke him up. "Quick, get up!" he said, and the chains fell off Peter's wrists. . . . "Wrap your cloak around you and follow me," the angel told him. . . . They passed the first and second guards and came to the iron gate leading to the city. It opened for them by itself, and they went through it. When they had walked the length of one street, suddenly the angel left him. Then Peter . . . said, "Now I know without a doubt that the Lord sent his angel and rescued me from Herod's clutches." (Acts 12:5-11, NIV)

TAKEAWAY
The Lord sent his angel and rescued me.

□ 224 _____

See, I am sending my angel before you to lead you safely to the land I have prepared for you. Pay attention to him, and obey all of his instructions. Do not rebel against him, for he will not forgive your sins. He is my representative—he bears my name. But if you are careful to obey him, following all my instructions, then I will be an enemy to your enemies, and I will oppose those who oppose you. For my angel will go before you and bring you into the land of the Amorites, Hittites, Perizzites, Canaanites, Hivites, and Jebusites, so you may live there. And I will destroy them. Do not worship the gods of these other nations or serve them in any way. . . . You must serve only the

Lord your God. If you do, I will bless you.
(Exodus 23:20-25)

I am sending my angel before you to lead you
safely to the land I have prepared for you.

MIND MENDER:

> *Angels, where ere we go,*
> *Attend our steps whate'er betide.*
> *With watchful care their charge attend,*
> *And evil turn aside.*
>
> —CHARLES WESLEY

Thirty-Three

TOUGHING IT OUT

☐ 225 _____

Because the Sovereign Lord helps me, I will not be
dismayed. Therefore, I have set my face like a
stone, determined to do his will. And I know that
I will triumph. He who gives me justice is near.
Who will dare to oppose me now? . . . See, the Sovereign Lord is on my side! . . . All my enemies will
be destroyed like old clothes that have been eaten
by moths! (Isaiah 50:7-9)

TAKEAWAY
**Because the Sovereign Lord helps me, I know
that I will triumph.**

☐ 226 _____

You should not be like cowering, fearful slaves.
You should behave instead like God's very own

children, adopted into his family—calling him "Father, dear Father." (Romans 8:15)

When I dwell on my weaknesses, I forget my Father's power.

□ 227 _____

Is anything too hard for the Lord? ❖ How can we understand the road we travel? It is the Lord who directs our steps. (Genesis 18:14; Proverbs 20:24)

TAKEAWAY
How can we understand the road we travel? It is the Lord who directs our steps.

□ 228 _____

God moves in a mysterious way His wonders to perform; ❖ He plants His footsteps in the sea, and rides upon the storm. ❖ Ye fearful saints, fresh courage take; the clouds ye so much dread ❖ Are big with mercy, and shall break in blessings on your head. —William Cowper, "God Moves in a Mysterious Way"

TAKEAWAY
The clouds ye so much dread are big with mercy and shall break in blessings on your head.

□ 229 _____

[The Lord] said, "My gracious favor is all you need. My power works best in your weakness." . . .

I am quite content with my weaknesses.... For when I am weak, then I am strong. (2 Corinthians 12:9-10)

TAKEAWAY

[The Lord] said, "I am with you; that is all you need."

☐ 230 _____

For the Lord God is our light and protector. He gives us grace and glory. No good thing will the Lord withhold from those who do what is right. (Psalm 84:11)

TAKEAWAY

We keep asking ourselves, "What will we do next?" We really need to ask, "What will God do next in our lives?" —Dr. Charles Allen, *You Are Never Alone*

☐ 231 _____

In quietness and confidence shall be your strength. ❖ Those that wait upon the Lord, they shall inherit the earth. (Isaiah 30:15; Psalm 37:9, KJV) This is no Pollyanna performance. This requires guts and courage and deep faith, and obedience of the toughest sort. —Rector of St. Thomas Church, New York City, *Day by Day*

TAKEAWAY

Somehow we never see God in failure, but only in success—a strange attitude for people who

have the cross as the center of their faith.
—Cheryl Forbes, *The Religion of Power*

MIND MENDER: Go forward, always go forward. You must not fall. Go until the last shots are fired and the last drop of gasoline is gone. Then go forward on foot.
—General George S. Patton

Thirty-Four

EACH DAY A NEW BEGINNING

O God, thou art my God; early will I seek thee:
my soul thirsteth for thee, my flesh longeth for
thee in a dry and thirsty land, where no water is;
to see thy power and thy glory, so as I have seen
thee in the sanctuary. Because thy lovingkindness
is better than life, my lips shall praise thee. Thus
will I bless thee while I live: I will lift up my
hands in thy name. My soul shall be satisfied as
with marrow and fatness; and my mouth shall
praise thee with joyful lips. (Psalm 63:1-5, KJV)

TAKEAWAY

> *Because the road is rough and long,*
> *Shall we despise the skylark's song?*
>
> —ANN BRONTE, *Views Of Life*

_____

Praise ye the Lord, Praise, O ye servants of the Lord, praise the name of the Lord. Blessed be the name of the Lord from this time forth and for evermore. From the rising of the sun unto the going down of the same the Lord's name is to be praised. The Lord is high above all nations, and his glory above the heavens. (Psalm 113:1-4, KJV)

TAKEAWAY
From the rising of the sun unto the going down of the same, the Lord's name is to be praised.

_____

> *I'm pressing on the upward way*
> *New heights I'm gaining every day*
> *Still praying as I'm onward bound,*
> *"Lord, plant my feet on higher ground."*
> —*JOHNSON OATMAN JR., "Higher Ground"*

TAKEAWAY
Each day I gain a little more of God's character and purposes. Each day, my spiritual journey takes me to higher ground.

_____

> *Each morning is a new beginning of our life.*
> *Each day is a finished whole.*
> *The present day marks the boundary*
> *of our cares and concerns.*
> *It is long enough to find God or to lose him,*
> *to keep faith*

or fall into disgrace.
God created day and night for us so we need not
wander without boundaries, but may be able
to see in every morning
the goal of the evening ahead.
Just as the ancient sun rises anew every day,
so the eternal mercy of God is new every morning.
Every morning God gives us
the gift of comprehending anew
his faithfulness of old;
thus, in the midst of our life with God,
we may daily begin a new life with him.
The first moments of the new day are for God's
liberating grace,
God's sanctifying presence.
Before the heart
unlocks itself for the world,
God wants to open it for himself;
before the ear takes in
the countless voices of the day,
it should hear in the early hours
the voice of the Creator and Redeemer.
God prepared the stillness
of the first morning
for himself.
It should remain his.

—*DIETRICH BONHOEFFER*

☐ 236 _____

Tears may linger at nightfall, but joy cometh in
the morning. ❖Why art thou cast down, O my
soul? and why art thou disquieted within me?

hope thou in God: for I shall yet praise him, who is the health of my countenance, and my God. (Psalms 30:5 NEB; 42:11, KJV)

TAKEAWAY

Why art thou cast down, O my soul? Joy cometh in the morning.

☐ 237 _____

This is the day which the Lord hath made; we will rejoice and be glad in it. ❖I will sing about your power. I will shout with joy each morning because of your unfailing love. For you have been my refuge, a place of safety in the day of distress. O my Strength, to you I sing praises, for you, O God, are my refuge, the God who shows me unfailing love. (Psalms 118:24, KJV; 59:16-17)

TAKEAWAY

I will sing about your power. I will shout with joy each morning because of your unfailing love.

☐ 238 _____

Thy righteousness is like the mountains of God; Thy judgments are like a great deep. O Lord, Thou preservest man and beast. How precious is Thy lovingkindness, O God! And the children of men take refuge in the shadow of Thy wings. They drink their fill of the abundance of Thy house; and Thou dost give them to drink of the river of Thy delights for with Thee is the fountain of life.

❖ Let us greet the dawn with song! O God, my heart is quiet and confident. No wonder I can sing your praises! Rouse yourself my soul! Thy lovingkindness, O Lord, extends to the heavens. Thy faithfulness reaches to the skies. (Psalms 36:5-9 NASB; 57:7-8)

TAKEAWAY
Rouse yourself, my soul! The Lord dost give his children to drink of the river of his delights.

MIND MENDER: The Lord gives me a light heart and a lovely day.

Thirty-Five

LORD, I'M TRYING TO
FORGIVE MYSELF

☐ 239 _____

In this man Jesus there is forgiveness for your sins.
Everyone who believes in him is freed from all
guilt and declared right with God. ❖ For you
know that God paid a ransom to save you. . . .
And the ransom he paid was not mere gold or silver. He paid for you with the precious lifeblood of
Christ, the sinless, spotless Lamb of God. (Acts
13:38-39; 1 Peter 1:18-19)

TAKEAWAY
Never build a case against yourself. It's OK to
have a past. We are all damaged persons. The
main thing is: Did you learn from it? Have you
determined to stop the behavior or attitude that
damaged God's wonderful creation (you!)?
Have you cleared out the guilt by confessing it
to God, and then have you claimed your life as
a clean slate, ready to start again?

"Come now, and let us reason together," says the
Lord. "Though your sins are as scarlet, they will be
as white as snow; though they are red like crim-
son, they will be like wool." . . . Truly, the mouth
of the Lord has spoken. (Isaiah 1:18-20, NASB)

TAKEAWAY
Think about it. Whiter than snow!

Rock of Ages, cleft for *ME*. ❖I felt that I did trust
in Christ, Christ alone for salvation; and an assurance was given me that He had taken away my
sins, even mine, and saved *me* from the law of sin
and death. —John Wesley

TAKEAWAY
> *No condemnation now I dread;*
> *Jesus, with all in him, is mine!*
> *Alive in Him, my living Head,*
> *And clothed in righteousness Divine,*
> *Bold I approach th'eternal throne,*
> *And claim the crown, thro' Christ my own.*
>
> —CHARLES WESLEY, *"And Can It Be That I Should Gain"*

Bless the Lord, O my soul; and all that is within
me, bless His holy name . . . who pardons all your
iniquities. ❖As high as the heavens are above the
earth, so great is His lovingkindness toward those
who fear Him. As far as the east is from the west,

so far has He removed our transgressions from us. (Psalm 103:1-3, 11-12, NASB)

I cannot experience peace as long as I keep on hassling God about whether or not He has completely forgiven me. Often, past badness that is already covered by Christ's blood comes to mind accusingly: "Surely God could not forget THAT sin," or "You have no right to enjoy life today because you hurt someone deeply back then." When those thoughts persist, I reply aloud, "Buzz off, Satan. Today, I am saying yes to my own righteousness." It works!
—Anonymous

☐ 243 _____

Now when sins have been forgiven, there is no need to offer any more sacrifices. And so, dear friends, we can boldly enter heaven's Most Holy Place because of the blood of Jesus. This is the new, life-giving way that Christ has opened up for us through the sacred curtain, by means of his death for us. (Hebrews 10:18-20)

T A K E A W A Y

Confessing sins does not mean begging and pleading for forgiveness. You bring the sins to God in an earnest way, then leave them there and claim the forgiveness provided 2,000 years ago. After that, get on with life. It seems so easy, but many find it so difficult! He really *is* Lord of the second chance.

You have undoubtedly had the experience of standing on the shore of a lake, or the ocean, on a moonlit night. The moon sends a silvery ray of light over the water directly to the place where you stand, as though it existed only for you. As you move, to right or left, the moonlight follows you, wherever you go along the beach. In somewhat the same way, God's forgiveness and love exist for you as if you were the only person on earth. They follow you, seek you out. You are not compelled to accept the gentle, unrelenting love that is being directed toward you. You have the choice—to ignore it, to think about it momentarily, or to dwell and revel in it. You may have as much of it as you wish. God awaits your response to his divine initiative. —Cecil Osborne, *The Joy of Understanding Your Faith*

TAKEAWAY
Lord, I did confess in all earnestness. My intention is not to repeat this transgression. Now, I thank you that you do not even remember what I am feeling guilty about.

Who dares accuse us whom God has chosen for his own? Will God? No! He is the one who has given us right standing with himself. Who then will condemn us? Will Christ Jesus? No, for he is the one who died for us and was raised to life for us and is sitting at the place of highest honor next to God, pleading for us. (Romans 8:33-34)

By condemning ourselves, we are saying that Christ's payment for our sins was not sufficient. As long as we substitute our standards and our reasonings in place of God's we are doomed to have problems with self-acceptance. It is just not possible for us to have a secure identity and a deep sense of personal worth until we accept the facts about us outlined in Scripture. But as soon as we understand and believe what Scripture says about us, we find a rich and enduring basis of self-acceptance. Take it easy on yourself. It takes a while to learn to experience God's forgiveness. —Bruce Narramore, *You're Someone Special*

MIND MENDER: Just having a sliver in my finger does not make me a totem pole.

Thirty-Six

GETTING MY THOUGHTS UNDER CONTROL

☐ 246 _____

Let the peace of God rule in your hearts. ❖ Be not conformed to this world, but be ye transformed by the renewing of your mind. ❖ Commit thy works unto the Lord, and thy thoughts shall be established. (Colossians 3:15; Romans 12:2; Proverbs 16:3, KJV)

TAKEAWAY
Christ comes to you and me in our lonely fear with all power and authority. He will not leave us helpless in the restless seas of life. Sometimes the Lord rides out the storm with us and

other times He calms the restless sea around us. Most of all, He calms the storm inside us in our deepest inner soul. And when He does, we can begin to face all the fears that disturb us in our thinking, in our personal relationships and responsibilities, and in our culture. —Dr. Lloyd Ogilvie, *12 Steps to Living without Fear*

☐ 247 _____

Have no fear; do not be dismayed, for the battle is in God's hand, not yours. (2 Chronicles 20:15, NEB)

TAKEAWAY

I was convinced I was losing my mind and descending into mental illness. Finally, I gave up. I told God I would accept a breakdown if something good could come of it. I began to understand that I was not losing my mind but rather that my poor mind was exhausted from fighting battles that were not mine to fight. Day by day, a thousand times at first, I would say, "It's not my problem."

I imagined myself in a small boat with God, riding an ocean of emotional turmoil. I accepted the waves and storms for as long as God would allow them, all the while resting in my little boat of safety, letting Him do it all for me. Struggling to rest in Him. . . . Isn't that the answer for all of us? . . . the key to the door marked EXIT? —a Christian mother, quoted in *Lifetime Guarantee* magazine, September 1994

_____

Set your mind on things above, not on earthly
things. ❖ Put to death whatever belongs to your
earthly nature. ❖ You must rid yourselves of all
such things as these: anger, rage, malice, slander,
and filthy language. ❖ As God's chosen people,
holy and dearly loved, clothe yourselves with compassion, kindness, humility, gentleness and
patience. Bear with each other and forgive whatever grievances you may have against one another.
Forgive as the Lord forgave you. ❖ And whatever
you do, whether in word or deed, do it all in the
name of the Lord Jesus. (Colossians 3:2, 5, 8,
12-13, 17, NIV)

TAKEAWAY
**Set your mind on things above, not on earthly
things.**

_____

I will pray with my spirit, but I will also pray with
my mind; I will sing with my spirit, but I will also
sing with my mind. ❖ O sing to the Lord a new
song. Make a joyful noise to the Lord all the earth;
break forth into joyous song and sing praises! Let
the sea roar, and all that fills it. Let the floods clap
their hands; let the hills sing for joy. ❖ Extol the
Lord our God; worship at his footstool! Holy is
he! (1 Corinthians 14:15, NIV; Psalms 98:1, 4-8;
99:5, RSV)

**Count your many blessings—name them one by
one, and it will surprise you what the Lord hath
done. —Johnson Oatman Jr., "Count Your
Blessings"**

☐ 250 _____

When I call thee to mind upon my bed and think
on thee in the watches of the night, remembering
how thou has been my help and that I am safe in
the shadow of thy wings, then I humbly follow
thee with all my heart, and thy right hand is my
support. (Psalm 63:6-8, NEB)

T A K E A W A Y

**When I follow God into the quiet places of
prayer and supplication, I will try to remember
that my Father owns the cattle on a thousand
hills, that he actually made those very lush hills,
that he has all power in heaven and earth. He is
my Divine Supplier, my Helper, and his plenti-
ful resources are my supply.**

☐ 251 _____

In thee I put my trust. ❖You have made wide
steps for my feet to keep them from slipping.
❖ You have given me strength for the battle and
have caused me to subdue all those who rose
against me. You have made my enemies turn
and run away. . . . You have preserved me.
(Psalm 143:8, RSV; 2 Samuel 22:37, 40-44)

What happens to me is not as important as my attitude toward what happens.

☐ 252 _____

Who shall separate us from the love of Christ?
Shall tribulation, or distress, or persecution, or
famine, or nakedness, or peril, or sword? No, in
all these things we are more than conquerors
through him who loved us. (Romans 8:35-37, RSV)

TAKEAWAY
**That man is perfect in faith who can come to
God in the utter dearth of his feelings and
desires, without a glow or an aspiration, with
the weight of low thoughts, failures, neglects,
and wandering forgetfulness, and say to Him,
"Thou art my refuge." —George Macdonald,
Unspoken Sermons, First Series, "The Child in the
Midst"**

MIND MENDER: Set your mind on biblical truths.
Force your mind to generate appropriate and true and
positive thoughts while refusing to accept negative
thoughts. Thinking thoughts that are true and real will
free up energy for constructive uses. Gently escort the
negatives out of your mind every time they return.
Keep at this five minutes, ten minutes, whatever time is
necessary until the negative "attack" eases off and your
emotions begin to settle down.

Thirty-Seven

I CAN TRUST A GOD LIKE THIS

☐ 253 _____

Oh, that you would burst from the heavens and come down! How the mountains would quake in your presence! As fire causes wood to burn and water to boil, your coming would make the nations tremble. . . . For since the world began, no ear has heard, and no eye has seen a God like you, who works for those who wait for him! (Isaiah 64:1-4)

TAKEAWAY
You placed the world on its foundation so it would never be moved. You clothed the earth with floods of water, water that covered even the mountains. At the sound of your rebuke, the water fled; at the sound of your thunder, it fled away. Mountains rose and valleys sank to the levels you decreed. Then you set a firm boundary

for the seas, so they would never again cover the earth. ❖ May the glory of the Lord last forever! The Lord rejoices in all he has made! (Psalm 104:5-9, 31)

☐ 254 _____

I am the Lord, the God of all the peoples of the world. Is anything too hard for me? ❖I alone am God, the First and the Last. It was my hand that laid the foundations of the earth. The palm of my right hand spread out the heavens above. I spoke, and they came into being. (Jeremiah 32:27; Isaiah 48:12-13)

TAKEAWAY
It was my hand that laid the foundations of the earth.

☐ 255 _____

It is the Lord who created the stars, the Pleiades and Orion. It is he who turns darkness into morning and day into night. It is he who draws up water from the oceans and pours it down as rain on the land. The Lord is his name! (Amos 5:8)

TAKEAWAY
It is the Lord who created the stars. It is he who turns darkness into morning and day into night.

☐ 256 _____

[He] . . . is the blessed and only Sovereign, the King of kings and Lord of lords, who alone has immortality and dwells in unapproachable light, whom no man has ever seen or can see. ❖Thy dominion endures throughout all generations. (1 Timothy 6:15-16, RSV; Psalm 145:13, NASB)

TAKEAWAY
He is the King of kings and Lord of lords.

☐ 257 _____

Who but God goes up to heaven and comes back down? Who holds the wind in his fists? Who wraps up the oceans in his cloak? Who has created the whole wide world? What is his name—and his son's name? Tell me if you know! (Proverbs 30:4)

TAKEAWAY
Who but God holds the wind in his fists? Who wraps up the oceans in his cloak?

☐ 258 _____

Look up into the heavens. Who created all the stars? He brings them out one after another, calling each by its name. And he counts them to see that none are lost or have strayed away. (Isaiah 40:26)

TAKEAWAY
Who created all the stars? He counts them to see that none are lost or have strayed away.

☐ 259 _____

Thine, O Lord, is the greatness and the power and the glory and the victory and the majesty, indeed everything that is in the heavens and the earth; Thine is the dominion, O Lord, and Thou dost exalt Thyself as head over all. Both riches and honor come from Thee, and Thou dost rule over all, and in Thy hand is power and might; and it lies in Thy hand to make great, and to strengthen everyone. Now therefore, our God, we thank Thee, and praise Thy glorious name. (1 Chronicles 29:11-13, NASB)

TAKEAWAY

Stop a minute and envision what might it took to blast life back into a dead body and then to lift it up out of a stone cave. Maybe the crisis you are experiencing right now is an opportunity to discover all that God is.

MIND MENDER: Surely, with all the benefits of taking the God-route through life, ignorance about his love and power to work in our behalf must be the most important reason so many people resist God.

Thirty-Eight

ANCHORED

☐ 260 _____

Blessed be the Lord, my rock and my fortress, my stronghold and my deliverer, my shield and He in whom I take refuge. ❖Those who trust in the Lord are as secure as Mount Zion; they will not be defeated but will endure forever. Just as the mountains surround and protect Jerusalem, so the Lord surrounds and protects his people. (Psalms 144:1-2, NASB; 125:1-2)

TAKEAWAY
Know my divine power. Trust in me. Dwell in my love. Seek safety in my secret place. You cannot be touched or harmed there. That is sure. Really feel as if you were in a strong tower,

strongly guarded, and against which nothing can prevail. —God speaking, in *God Calling*, edited by A. J. Russell

☐ 261 _____

"His eye is on the sparrow, and I know he watches me." —sung by Cliff Barrows at Billy Graham Crusades

TAKEAWAY
A God whose presence and scrutiny I could evade would be a small and trivial diety. Every moment of life is spent in the sight and company of an omniscient, omnipresent Creator. This is momentous knowledge. There is unspeakable comfort—the sort that energizes and enervates—knowing that God is constantly taking knowledge of me in love, and watching over me for my good. —J. I. Packer, *Knowing God*

☐ 262 _____

With God's help we shall do mighty things. ❖I will cry to you for help, for my heart is overwhelmed. Lead me to the towering rock of safety, for you are my safe refuge, a fortress where my enemies cannot reach me. ❖The Lord lives! Blessed be my rock! May the God of my salvation be exalted! (Psalms 60:12; 61:2-3; 18:46)

TAKEAWAY
Blessed be my rock! May the God of my salvation be exalted!

David sang this song to the Lord after the Lord had rescued him from all his enemies and from Saul . . . : "The Lord is my rock, my fortress, and my savior; my God is my rock, in whom I find protection. He is my shield, the strength of my salvation, and my stronghold, my high tower, my savior, the one who saves me from violence. I will call on the Lord, who is worthy of praise, for he saves me from my enemies. "The waves of death surrounded me; the floods of destruction swept over me. The grave wrapped its ropes around me; death itself stared me in the face. But in my distress I cried out to the Lord; yes, I called to my God for help. He heard me from his sanctuary; my cry reached his ears. "Then the earth quaked and trembled; the foundations of the heavens shook; they quaked because of his anger. Smoke poured from his nostrils; fierce flames leaped from his mouth; glowing coals flamed forth from him. He opened the heavens and came down; dark storm clouds were beneath his feet. Mounted on a mighty angel, he flew, soaring on the wings of the wind. He shrouded himself in darkness, veiling his approach with dense rain clouds. A great brightness shone before him, and bolts of lightning blazed forth. The Lord thundered from heaven; the Most High gave a mighty shout. He shot his arrows and scattered his enemies; his lightning flashed, and they were confused. Then at the command of the Lord, at the blast of his breath, the bottom of the sea could be seen, and the foundations of the earth were laid bare. "He reached down from heaven and rescued me; he drew me out of deep waters. He delivered me from my powerful enemies, from those who hated me and were too strong for me. They attacked me at a moment when I was weakest, but the Lord upheld me. He led me to a place of safety; he rescued me because he delights in me." (2 Samuel 22:1-20)

TAKEAWAY
He rescued me because he delights in me.

☐ 264 _____

She was in a wheelchair and came weekly to my seminar on "Making Your Marriage Sparkle." Tubes came from everywhere in her small, fragile body, and they led to several bottles attached beneath her chair. One paralyzed hand lay lifeless on the tray; her withered legs had not been used in years. She had multiple sclerosis. ❖ "How *do* you handle it?" asked one of the six other women gathered around her wheelchair during the seminar break. With the most gracious and understanding smile, she paused a long moment and then quietly and slowly told them, "Only my body is wasting away. I am a child of the King of kings. That is enough. There is peace like a river in my soul." ❖ Tears filled every eye as her peace overflowed to each one of us. "She knows what being anchored in the love of Christ is all about," I thought.

I am wholly His; I am peculiarly His; I am universally His; I am eternally His. —Thomas Brooks, *The Golden Treasury of Puritan Quotations*

□ 265 _____

O Lord, you are my light; yes, Lord, you light up my darkness. In your strength I can crush an army; with my God I can scale any wall. . . . He is a shield for all who look to him for protection. For who is God except the Lord? Who but our God is a solid rock? . . . He makes me as surefooted as a deer, leading me safely along the mountain heights. (2 Samuel 22:29-34)

TAKEAWAY
He makes me as surefooted as a deer, leading me safely along the mountain heights.

□ 266 _____

I give you thanks, O Lord, with all my heart. ❖ Though I am surrounded by troubles, you will preserve me against the anger of my enemies. You will clench your fist against my angry enemies! Your power will save me. The Lord will work out his plans for my life—for your faithful love, O Lord, endures forever. Don't abandon me, for you made me. (Psalm 138:1, 7-8)

The Lord will work out his plans for my life—
for your faithful love, O Lord, endures forever.
You made me.

MIND MENDER:

*Though the angry surges roll
On my tempest-driven soul,
I am peaceful, for I know,
Wildly though the winds may blow,
I've an anchor safe and sure,
That can evermore endure.*

*Mighty tides about me sweep,
Perils lurk within the deep,
Angry clouds o'ershade the sky,
And the tempest rises high;
Still I stand the tempest's shock,
For my anchor grips the Rock.*

*And it holds, my anchor holds;
Blow your wildest then, O gale,
On my bark so small and frail;
By His grace I shall not fail,
For my anchor holds.
My anchor holds.*

—W. C. MARTIN, "My Anchor Holds"

Thirty-Nine

WHY AM I HERE?

☐ 267

He has showed you, O man, what is good. What does the Lord require of you? To act justly and to love mercy and to walk humbly with your God. ❖ Be ye doers of the word, and not hearers only. ❖ As the elect of God, holy and beloved, put on tender mercies, kindness, humility, meekness, longsuffering; bearing with one another, and forgiving one another. (Micah 6:8, NIV; James 1:22, KJV; Colossians 3:12-13, NKJV)

TAKEAWAY
What does the Lord require of you? To act justly and to love mercy and to walk humbly with your God.

We are God's workmanship, created in Christ Jesus to do good works, which God prepared in advance for us to do. ❖ May the Lord make you increase and abound in love to one another. (Ephesians 2:10, NIV; 1 Thessalonians 3:12, NKJV)

TAKEAWAY

> *If I can stop one Heart from breaking*
> *I shall not live in vain.*
> *If I can ease one Life the Aching*
> *Or cool one Pain,*
> *Or help one fainting Robin*
> *Unto his Nest again*
> *I shall not live in Vain.*

—EMILY DICKINSON, *"If I Can Stop One Heart from Breaking"*

Early the next morning Jesus went out into the wilderness. The crowds searched everywhere for him, and when they finally found him, they begged him not to leave them. But he replied, "I must preach the Good News of the Kingdom of God in other places, too, because that is why I was sent." So he continued to travel around, preaching in synagogues throughout Judea. (Luke 4:42-44)

TAKEAWAY

We are Christs to our neighbor. —Martin Luther

_____

I want you to be merciful; I don't want your sacrifices. I want you to know God; that's more important than burnt offerings. ❖This is what the Lord says: "Let not the wise man gloat in his wisdom, or the mighty man in his might, or the rich man in his riches. Let them boast in this alone: that they truly know me and understand that I am the Lord who is just and righteous, whose love is unfailing, and that I delight in these things." (Hosea 6:6; Jeremiah 9:23-24)

TAKEAWAY

What were we made for? To know God. What aim should we set ourselves in life? To know God. What is the "eternal life" that Jesus gives? Knowledge of God. "This is life eternal, that they might know thee, the only true God, and Jesus Christ, whom thou hast sent " (John 17:3, KJV).

☐ 271 _____

"Of all the commandments, which is the most important?" Jesus replied, "The most important commandment is this: 'Hear, O Israel! The Lord our God is the one and only Lord. And you must love the Lord your God with all your heart, all your soul, all your mind, and all your strength.' The second is equally important: 'Love your neighbor as yourself.' No other commandment is greater than these." (Mark 12:28-31)

Resolved: that all men should live for the glory of God. Resolved second: that whether others do or not, I will. —Jonathan Edwards, *Seventy Resolutions*

☐ 272 _____

But may all who search for you be filled with joy and gladness. May those who love your salvation repeatedly shout, "The Lord is great!" ❖ And so, since God in his mercy has given us this wonderful ministry, we never give up. ❖ With Jesus' help, let us continually offer our sacrifice of praise to God by proclaiming the glory of his name. (Psalm 40:16; 2 Corinthians 4:1; Hebrews 13:15)

T A K E A W A Y
The lips of the righteous feed many. (Proverbs 10:21, KJV)

☐ 273 _____

If I could speak in any language in heaven or on earth but didn't love others, I would only be making meaningless noise. . . . And if I had the gift of faith so that I could speak to a mountain and make it move, without love I would be no good to anybody. (1 Corinthians 13:1-2)

T A K E A W A Y
If I had the gift of faith so that I could speak to a mountain and make it move, without love I would be no good to anybody.

Once you become aware that the main business that you are here for is to know God, most of life's problems fall into place of their own accord. What makes life worthwhile is having a big enough objective, something which catches our imagination and lays hold of our allegiance; and this the Christian has, in a way that no other man has. For what higher, more exalted and more compelling goal can there be than to know God? —J. I. Packer, *Knowing God*

Forty

LORD, I FEEL SO SICK

☐ 274 _____

I pray with all my heart; answer me, Lord! . . . I
rise early, before the sun is up; I cry out for help
and put my hope in your words. I stay awake
through the night, thinking about your promise.
In your faithful love, O Lord, hear my cry; in your
justice, save my life. (Psalm 119:145-149)

TAKEAWAY
**I rise early, before the sun is up; I cry out for
help and put my hope in your words.**

☐ 275 _____

You made my body, Lord. . . . Now, let your lovingkindness comfort me. . . . Surround me with your

tender mercies. . . . I will concentrate my thoughts upon your laws. ❖ He will show compassion, so great is his unfailing love. For he does not willingly bring affliction or grief to the children of men. (Psalm 119:73-78; Lamentations 3:32-33, NIV)

TAKEAWAY
You created me, Lord. Then you re-created me and I became yours through the blood of Christ. I know that you can do it again, my heavenly Father.

☐ 276 _____

Jesus went about all Galilee, teaching in their synagogues, and preaching the gospel of the kingdom, and healing all manner of sickness and all manner of disease among the people. They brought unto him all sick people that were taken with divers diseases and torments, and those which were possessed with devils, and those which were lunatick, and those that had the palsy; and he healed them. And there followed him great multitudes of people. (Matthew 4:23-25, KJV)

TAKEAWAY
Jesus Christ the same yesterday, and to day, and for ever. (Hebrews 13:8, KJV)

☐ 277 _____

We are often troubled, but not crushed; sometimes in doubt, but never in despair; there are many enemies, but we are never without a friend. (2 Corinthians 4:8-9, TEV)

We are never without a friend.

□ 278 _____

Jesus beheld them, and said unto them, "With men this is impossible; but with God all things are possible." (Matthew 19:26, KJV)

As you pray for health, remember that you are to see only health and perfection. You are to behold God's perfect manifestation of life and health. Instead of focusing your attention on the condition as it appears, try to keep your thoughts centered in God. Take time to feel the power of God stirring within you. Believe that God is doing his healing work now. Feel God's presence with you, lifting you up, and filling your heart with the deep and abiding assurance that all is well. —Dr. Norman Vincent Peale, *Healing*

□ 279 _____

I love the Lord, for he heard my voice; he heard my cry for mercy. Because he turned his ear to me, I will call on him as long as I live. The cords of death entangled me, the anguish of the grave came upon me; I was overcome by trouble and sorrow. Then I called on the name of the Lord:

"O Lord, save me!" The Lord is gracious and righteous; our God is full of compassion. The Lord protects the simplehearted; when I was in great need, he saved me. Be at rest once more, O my soul, for the Lord has been good to you. (Psalm 116:1-7, NIV)

TAKEAWAY
How unsearchable are his judgments and his ways past finding out! (Romans 11:33, NEB)

☐ 280 _____

I will not forget you! See, I have engraved you on the palms of my hands. ❖Hallelujah! For our Lord God Almighty reigns. Let us rejoice and be glad and give him glory! (Isaiah 49:15-16; Revelation 19:6-7, NIV)

TAKEAWAY
Our God reigns! He is King of kings and Lord of lords. Our God reigns!

MIND MENDER: He understands my agony. When I suffer, I better understand his.

Forty-One

HIS PAIN, MY PAIN

☐ 281 _____

Because God's children are human beings—made
of flesh and blood—Jesus also became flesh and
blood by being born in human form. For only as
a human being could he die, and only by dying
could he break the power of the Devil, who had
the power of death. . . . It was necessary for Jesus
to be in every respect like us, his brothers and sisters. . . . Since he himself has gone through suffering and temptation, he is able to help us when we
are being tempted. (Hebrews 2:14-18)

TAKEAWAY
**Since he himself has gone through suffering
and temptation, he is able to help us when we
are being tempted.**

If you suffer for doing good and you endure it,
this is commendable before God. . . . Christ suffered for you, leaving you an example, that you
should follow in his steps. (1 Peter 2:20-21, NIV)

TAKEAWAY

See, from His head, His hands, His feet,
Sorrow and love flow mingled down.

—ISAAC WATTS, "When I Survey the Wondrous Cross"

Jesus must have felt like the world was closing in.
He knew and understood what death on a cross
involved. The physical humiliation and agony of
crucifixion would only be compounded by the
horror of experiencing God's wrath for the sins of
the world. There was only one solution for deal-
ing with the feelings welling up inside him—
prayer. So, Jesus went alone to the Garden of
Gethsemane to pour out his heart to the Father.
Where do you go when life seems unbearable,
when stress is stretching every fiber of your being
to the maximum? Jesus identifies with your pain
and trial; he knows what it's like to be overwhelmed with conflicting emotions. But, think
about this: The worst problem you will ever face is
nothing compared to what Jesus went through.
And Jesus, who is God himself, handled his
ordeal on earth by going to the Father in private
prayer. —Dr. Charles Stanley, "The Battle Is Won"
(taped message)

Let us draw near [to God] with a true heart in full assurance of faith. ❖Commune with your own heart upon your bed, and be still. (Hebrews 10:22; Psalm 4:4, KJV)

☐ 284 _____

Blessed be God, even the Father of our Lord Jesus Christ, the Father of mercies, and the God of all comfort; who comforteth us in all our tribulation, that we may be able to comfort them which are in any trouble, by the comfort wherewith we ourselves are comforted of God. For as the sufferings of Christ abound in us, so our consolation also aboundeth by Christ. (2 Corinthians 1:3-5, KJV)

TAKEAWAY
Sufferings are but as little chips of the cross.
—Joseph Church, *The Golden Treasury of Puritan Quotations*

☐ 285 _____

Christ is the head of the church, which is his body. He is the first of all who will rise from the dead, so he is first in everything. For God in all his fullness was pleased to live in Christ. ❖[He] was incarnate of the Holy Spirit and the Virgin Mary, and was made man; and was crucified also for us under Pontius Pilate, and suffered and was buried; and the third day he rose again, according to the Scriptures; and ascended into heaven, and sitteth at the right hand of the Father. ❖[Jesus said,]

"Truly, you will weep and mourn over what is going to happen to me, but the world will rejoice. You will grieve, but your grief will suddenly turn to wonderful joy when you see me again. It will be like a woman experiencing the pains of labor. When her child is born, her anguish gives place to joy. ❖ I have told you all this so that you may have peace in me. Here on earth you will have many trials and sorrows. But take heart, because I have overcome the world." (Colossians 1:18-19; the Nicene Creed; John 16:20-21, 33)

TAKEAWAY

**To my dearly beloved children,
I understand. I really do.—God**

☐ 286 _____

I have loved you with an everlasting love; I have drawn you with loving-kindness. ❖ Let us not give up meeting together, as some are in the habit of doing, but let us encourage one another. (Jeremiah 31:3; Hebrews 10:25, NIV)

TAKEAWAY

Lord, sometimes I forget how much you must want to be with me and with your other beloved children. Let's you and me get together first thing tomorrow morning in a quiet place. I will allow you to encourage me as only you can do. I will listen as you whisper to me, "I know what suffering is like. I've been there." You can tell me once again the words I yearn to hear: "I love you just because

I made you, just because you exist." And then I will tell you how much I love you for being the suffering servant.

□ 287

How did our Lord suffer? ❖Author Corrie ten Boom, writing about her awful experiences in a Nazi concentration camp, notes that being stripped of her clothes and having to stand naked were the worst moments of all, even more degrading and torturous than being without food or living with filth and lice or being forced into hard, hard labor or having cruel guards beat her. She says that in those worst moments, she remembered that Jesus hung naked on the cross after his garments were taken away. "By my own suffering, I understood a fraction of Jesus' suffering," she says. ❖Jesus and other sufferers have much in common. They are both partakers of the same bitter cup. The result is mutual understanding. There is greater compassion and awareness of what toughness it takes to go through pain than with those who have never endured it. Perhaps, in a small sense, following the Lord in suffering is a privilege because it may be the one way we can experience this deeper understanding of just how much torment Jesus went through on that Black Friday, the only way I can get a true feel of the Cross experience.

What we suffer now is nothing compared to the glory he will give us later. (Romans 8:18)

MIND MENDER: When I suffer, I can better understand my Lord's suffering.

Forty-Two

I FEEL I'VE BEEN
TREATED UNJUSTLY

□ 288 _____

Your throne, O God, endures forever. Justice is
your royal scepter. (Psalm 45:6, NASB)

T A K E A W A Y
O God, justice is your royal scepter.

□ 289 _____

"Vengeance is Mine, I will repay," says the Lord.
❖ If your enemy is hungry, give him bread to eat;
and if he is thirsty, give him water to drink; for so
you will heap coals of fire on his head, and the
Lord will reward you. (Hebrews 10:30; Proverbs
25:21-22, NKJV)

T A K E A W A Y
"Vengeance is Mine, I will repay," says the Lord.

□ 290 _____

O Lord, it is good to give thee thanks . . . to
declare thy constancy every night. ❖ How fathomless thy thoughts! ❖ Though the wicked grow like
grass and every evildoer prospers, they will be
destroyed for ever. While thou, Lord, dost reign on
high eternally, thy foes will surely perish, all evil-
doers will be scattered. ❖ I listen for the downfall
of my cruel foes . . . eager to declare that the Lord
is just. (Psalm 92:1-2, 5, 7-9, 11, NEB)

T A K E A W A Y
O Lord, how fathomless thy thoughts!

□ 291 _____

The godly will rejoice when they see injustice
avenged. They will wash their feet in the blood of
the wicked. Then at last everyone will say, "There
truly is a reward for those who live for God; surely
there is a God who judges justly here on earth."
(Psalm 58:10-11)

T A K E A W A Y
There is a God who judges justly here on earth.

□ 292 _____

I saw the dead, small and great, stand before God;
and the books were opened . . . : and the dead were
judged out of those things which were written in the
books, according to their works. And the sea gave up
the dead which were in it; and death and hell delivered up the dead which were in them: and they were

judged every man according to their works. And death and hell were cast into the lake of fire. This is the second death. And whosoever was not found written in the book of life was cast into the lake of fire. (Revelation 20:12-15, KJV)

TAKEAWAY

Let justice roll down like waters, and righteousness like an everflowing stream. (Amos 5:24, RSV)

☐ 293 _____

Don't worry about the wicked. Don't envy those who do wrong. For like grass, they soon fade away. Like springtime flowers, they soon wither. Trust in the Lord and do good. . . . Commit everything you do to the Lord. Trust him, and he will help you. He will make your innocence as clear as the dawn, and the justice of your cause will shine like the noonday sun. Be still in the presence of the Lord, and wait patiently for him to act. . . . Stop your anger! Turn from your rage! Do not envy others—it only leads to harm. For the wicked will be destroyed, but those who trust in the Lord will possess the land. In a little while, the wicked will disappear. Though you look for them, they will be gone. Those who are gentle and lowly will possess the land; they will live in prosperous security. (Psalm 37:1-11)

TAKEAWAY

In the span of just a few hours, Jesus knew that he would be betrayed, denied, mocked, rejected, and crucified. Even with the hideousness of the

cross facing him, he refused to become bitter.
His eyes were leveled on one thing only—the
good and perfect will of the heavenly Father.
 —Dr. Charles Stanley, "When Others Fail Us"
(taped message)

□ 294 _____

The wicked plot against the godly; they snarl at them
in defiance. But the Lord just laughs, for he sees their
day of judgment coming. (Psalm 37:12-13)

T A K E A W A Y

**God is the King of all the earth. . . . God
reigneth over the heathen: God sitteth upon the
throne of his holiness. (Psalm 47:7-8, KJV)**

MIND MENDER: I'm glad that my heavenly Father
does not ask that I rejoice over all the circumstances
that come into my life. He asks only that I find joy even
in the midst of them.

Forty-Three

TAKE COURAGE,
MY SOUL

☐ 295 _____

Fear not, nor be dismayed, be strong and of good
courage. ❖ Be strong and courageous; be not
afraid nor dismayed. ❖ Watch ye, stand fast in the
faith, quit you like men, be strong. ❖ Be strong in
the Lord, and in the power of his might. ❖ Cast
thy burden upon the Lord, and he shall sustain
thee. ❖ In quietness and in confidence shall be
your strength. ❖ He giveth power to the faint; and
to them that have no might he increaseth
strength. (Joshua 10:25; 2 Chronicles 32:7;
1 Corinthians 16:13; Ephesians 6:10; Psalm 55:22;
Isaiah 30:15; 40:29, KJV)

TAKEAWAY
**Sometimes I go whistling down the road after
asking God the way.**

□ 296 _____

The Lord is king! Let the nations tremble! He sits on his throne between the cherubim. Let the whole earth quake! ❖ Mighty king, lover of justice, you have established fairness. You have acted with justice and righteousness. ❖ But God is my helper. The Lord is the one who keeps me alive! (Psalms 99:1, 4; 54:4)

T A K E A W A Y

God is my helper. The Lord is the one who keeps me alive!

□ 297 _____

It is no longer I who live, but Christ lives in me. (Galatians 2:20, NASB)

T A K E A W A Y

The resources of the Christian life are just Jesus Christ. —Charles Trumbull

□ 298 _____

For God is working in you, giving you the desire to obey him and the power to do what pleases him. ❖ Great is the Lord, who enjoys helping his servant. (Philippians 2:13; Psalm 35:27)

T A K E A W A Y

God is working in you, giving you the power to do what pleases him.

□ 299 _____

So take a new grip with your tired hands and stand
firm on your shaky legs. Mark out a straight path for
your feet. Then those who follow you, though they
are weak and lame, will not stumble and fall but
will become strong. ❖I work very hard at this, as I
depend on Christ's mighty power that works within
me. (Hebrews 12:12-13; Colossians 1:29)

TAKEAWAY
**There is pow'r, pow'r, wonder-working pow'r in
the precious blood of the Lamb. —Lewis E.
Jones, "There Is Power in the Blood"**

□ 300 _____

If the Lord had not been on our side . . . when
people rose up against us, they would have swallowed us alive because of their burning anger
against us. The waters would have engulfed us. . . .
The raging waters of their fury would have overwhelmed our very lives. Blessed be the Lord, who
did not let their teeth tear us apart! We escaped like
a bird from a hunter's trap. The trap is broken, and
we are free! Our help is from the Lord, who made
the heavens and the earth. (Psalm 124:1-8)

TAKEAWAY
Think about it. Heaven and earth!

□ 301 _____

O God:
Give me strength to live another day;

Let me not turn coward before its difficulties or
  prove recreant to its duties;
Let me not lose faith in other people;
Keep me sweet and sound of heart, in spite of
  ingratitude, treachery, or meanness;
Preserve me from minding little stings or giving
  them;
Help me to keep my heart clean, and to live so
  honestly and fearlessly that no outward
  failure can dishearten me or take away the
  joy of conscious integrity;
Open wide the eyes of my soul that I may see
  good in all things.
Grant me this day some new vision of thy truth;
Inspire me with the spirit of joy and gladness;
And make me the cup of strength to suffering
  souls;
In the name of the strong Deliverer,
our only Lord and Savior, Jesus Christ.

—PHILLIPS BROOKS, *quoted in devotional* Day by Day

TAKEAWAY
**O God, let me not turn coward toward the diffi-
culties of the day.**

MIND MENDER: Faith is the daring of the soul to go
farther than it can see. —William Newton Clark

Forty-Four

PRESCRIPTIONS FOR
A QUIET HEART

☐ 302 _____

But the Lord is my fortress; my God is a mighty
rock where I can hide. ❖For Christ has entered
into heaven itself to appear now before God as
our Advocate. (Psalm 94:22; Hebrews 9:24)

TAKEAWAY

**Quiet minds cannot be perplexed or frightened
but go on in fortune or in misfortune at their
own private pace like the ticking of a clock during a thunderstorm. —Robert Louis Stevenson**

☐ 303 _____

My friends, all that is true, all that is noble, all that
is just and pure, all that is lovable and gracious,
whatever is excellent and admirable—fill all your

thoughts with these things . . . and the God of
peace will be with you. (Philippians 4:8-9, NEB)

TAKEAWAY
**Fill your thoughts with positive things, and the
peace of God will be with you.**

□ 304 _____

Yea though I walk through the valley of the
shadow of death, I will fear no evil. ❖ I am yours!
. . . I have applied myself to obey your commandments. Though the wicked hide along the way to
kill me, I will quietly keep my mind on your
decrees. ❖ I have stilled and quieted myself, just as
a small child . . . is my soul within me. (Psalms
23:4, KJV; 119:94-95; 131:2)

TAKEAWAY
**I will quietly keep my mind upon your
promises.**

□ 305 _____

> *Like a river glorious is God's perfect peace,*
> *Over all victorious, in its bright increase;*
> *Perfect yet it floweth, fuller every day,*
> *Perfect yet it groweth, deeper all the way.*
>
> *Stayed upon Jehovah,*
> *Hearts are fully blest,*
> *Finding as He promised,*
> *Perfect peace and rest.*

Hidden in the hollow of His blessed hand,
Never foe can follow, never traitor stand;
Not a surge of worry, not a shade of care,
Not a blast of hurry touch the spirit there.

—FRANCES R. HAVERGAL, *"Like a River Glorious"*

TAKEAWAY

Hidden in the hollow of his blessed hand, not a surge of worry nor a shade of care can touch me there.

☐ 306 _____

Thou wilt keep him in perfect peace, whose mind is stayed on thee: because he trusteth in thee. (Isaiah 26:3, KJV)

TAKEAWAY

I know whom I have believed and am persuaded that he is able.

☐ 307 _____

Trust in the Lord with all thine heart and lean not unto thine own understanding. In all thy ways acknowledge him, and he shall direct thy paths. (Proverbs 3:5-6, KJV)

TAKEAWAY

A squirrel decided to make a break for the other side of the road in front of my car. He didn't make it. His hind legs were badly hurt, and he was bleeding internally. Carefully, I picked him up and carried him over to the thick carpet of grass beside the road and knelt beside him.

His muscles were hard, and his sharp claws scratched into the skin of my hands and wrists. His ears laid back against his head in a display of uncertainty, and there was abject terror in his shiny black eyes. I wanted to touch and comfort him, but he shrank from each move I made. I spoke to him softly and with reassuring words straight from my aching, empathetic heart—but to no avail. After a few moments, pulling himself on his belly across the grass, dragging his back legs behind him, the squirrel crawled toward a hedge, leaving me kneeling on the lawn in bankrupt grief at the scenario I was sure would soon follow.

I looked down at my hands spotted with blood, then out at the wounded squirrel. In an instant the scene changed. Suddenly I was in the place of the untrusting squirrel, wounded but dragging myself by my fingernails from the presence of God. I looked past my distrust into the eyes of this figure kneeling beside me and for the first time caught a glimpse of God's heart. Because of where I had knelt and the blood on my hands, I understood where God knelt and how He felt about the blood shed from His hands.

I understood! The emotion and distrust and skepticism of preceding years began to flow out of me. He is trustworthy!

Trust declares confidence in the Father even though He appears untrustworthy, even though it appears He has abandoned ship. —Preston Gillham, *Lifetime Guarantee* magazine

Sing to God, you kingdoms of the earth. Sing praises to the Lord. Sing to the one who rides across the ancient heavens, his mighty voice thundering from the sky. Tell everyone about God's power. . . . God is awesome in his sanctuary. [He] gives power and strength to his people. Praise be to God! (Psalm 68:32-35)

TAKEAWAY

Ask God to help you believe the incredible power He has ready to help you. Be still and ponder who God is each day.

MIND MENDER: Jesus didn't forbid wise planning; he did forbid useless worry.

Aspiration, a monthly devotional magazine, suggests making a list of things in your life you *do* control; then making another list of things in your life you *don't* control. Perhaps the first list includes prayer, quiet time, work, and other choices. Perhaps the second includes another person's attitude, a child's behavior, the weather, and future world events.

In the words of Reinhold Niebuhr, ask God to grant you serenity to accept the things you can't change (the second list), courage to change the things you can (the first list), and the wisdom to know the difference.

Forty-Five

LORD, I FEEL SO BROKEN

☐ 309 _____

My presence shall go with thee and I will give thee rest. (Exodus 33:14, KJV)

T A K E A W A Y

A businessman under great stress came to our church clinic complaining of severe nervousness. He drummed his fingers on my desk as he said, "I worry about my business all the time. Every time I am away I worry whether my house is going to burn down or something will happen to it. I worry about my wife and children, wondering if they are going to get hurt."

"Imagine that Jesus Christ is actually by your side," I told him. "When you start worrying, stop and say, 'Lord, You are with me; everything is all right.' When you go into a restaurant, even

195

if you are with somebody, pull up a chair and imagine that Jesus Christ sits in that chair. When you walk down the street, imagine that you can hear His footfalls, feel His shoulders, see His face. When you retire at night, pull up a chair by the bed and imagine that Jesus Christ sits in that chair. Then before you turn out the light say, 'Lord, I'll not worry, for I know that You are watching over me and will give me peace.'" —Dr. Norman Vincent Peale, *Guide to Confident Living*

☐ 310 _____

God is not a God of disorder but of peace. (1 Corinthians 14:33, NIV)

TAKEAWAY

Children and animals are scrupulously careful about doing exactly what they are doing at any given moment. I have never met an adult who dozes as skillfully as my cat. Nor do I know a man or woman my age who can swing with the same devotion as my son. Nothing distracts him. When he swings, he swings; when he sleeps, he sleeps. If I can acquire this new learning from my son, who sleeps so soundly when he sleeps, I will possess once again a kind of luxury no money can ever buy. —Tony Simmons, *The Christian Science Monitor*

Lord, help me to concentrate on just one thing at a time to keep from feeling so broken and fragmented.

☐ 311 _____

Though he slay me, yet will I trust him. (Job 13:15, KJV)

TAKEAWAY
> Be still, my soul: thy God doth undertake
> To guide the future as He has the past.
> Thy hope, thy confidence let nothing shake;
> All now mysterious shall be bright at last.

—KATHARINA VON SCHLEGEL, "Be Still, My Soul"

☐ 312 _____

Set your troubled hearts at rest. Trust in God always; trust also in Me. (John 14:1, NEB)

TAKEAWAY
Say aloud: "It is OK to have a good day even if there are lots of problems everywhere. God never meant me to feel frustrated and frazzled so much of the time."

☐ 313 _____

Ye are complete in Him. (Colossians 2:10, KJV)

TAKEAWAY
Peace (wholeness) has something to do with being able to stop all the struggling, and finally, just being able to let one's self be. Just to be. Fully and freely, unfettered and with wholeness. To be able to relax and be all right. To take a deep breath and lean back and sigh and BE and have it somehow be just fine. To rest. —Dr. Gerald D. May

Feeling broken and empty? Claim your completeness in him.

☐ 314 _____

We were harassed at every turn—conflicts on the outside, fears within. But God, who comforts the downcast, comforted us. (2 Corinthians 7:5-6, NIV)

TAKEAWAY
Faith is to believe what you do not yet see; the reward for this faith is to see what you believe. —St. Augustine
   Faith is the substance of things hoped for, the evidence of things not seen. (Hebrews 11:1, KJV)

☐ 315 _____

> *Drop Thy still dews of quietness,*
> *Till all our strivings cease;*
> *Take from our souls the strain and stress,*
> *And let our ordered lives confess*
> *The beauty of Thy peace.*
>
> —*JOHN G. WHITTIER, "Dear Lord and Father of Mankind"*

TAKEAWAY
Drop Thy still dews of quietness, till all our strivings cease.

MIND MENDER:
> *Blessed quietness, holy quietness,*
> *What assurance in my soul!*

On the stormy sea He speaks peace to me,
How the billows cease to roll!

—MANIE P. FERGUSON, *"Blessed Quietness"*

Forty-Six

TRYING TO TRUST

☐ 316 _____

"I am the Alpha and the Omega," says the Lord God, "who is, and who was, and who is to come, the Almighty." (Revelation 1:8, NIV)

TAKEAWAY
The same God who called Abraham, performed miracles through Elijah, and gave young Virgin Mary the Christ child works in our lives today.

☐ 317 _____

Never wait for fitter time or place to talk to Him. To wait till thou go to church or to thy closet is to make Him wait. He will listen as thou walkest.
—George Macdonald

TAKEAWAY
Open my eyes, that I may see
Glimpses of truth Thou hast for me;

Place in my hands the wonderful key
That shall unclasp, and set me free.

Silently now I wait for Thee,
Ready, my God, Thy will to see;
Open my eyes, illumine me,
Spirit divine!

—CLARA H. SCOTT, "Open My Eyes, That I May See"

☐ 318 _____

"To whom will you compare me? Who is my equal?" asks the Holy One. Look up into the heavens. Who created all the stars? He brings them out one after another, calling each by its name. And he counts them to see that none are lost or have strayed away. ❖ Who but God goes up to heaven and comes back down? Who holds the wind in his fists? Who wraps up the oceans in his cloak? Who has created the whole wide world? What is his name—and his son's name? Tell me if you know! (Isaiah 40:25-26; Proverbs 30:4)

TAKEAWAY
Say aloud once per hour all day today: "The God who rules the universe is the God who's holding me."

☐ 319 _____

I live my life in this earthly body by trusting in the Son of God, who loved me and gave himself for me. ❖ The Lord is close to all who call on him, yes, to all who call on him sincerely. He fulfills the desires of those who fear him; he hears their cries for help and rescues them. The Lord protects all those who love him, but he destroys the wicked. (Galatians 2:20; Psalm 145:18-20)

TAKEAWAY

It is not passionate appeal that gains the Divine Ear so much as the quiet placing of the difficulty and worry in Divine Hands. So trust and be no more afraid than a child would be, who places its tangled skein of wool in the hands of a loving mother, and runs out to play, pleasing the mother more by its unquestioning confidence than if it went down on its knees and implored her help, which would pain her rather, as it would imply she was not eager to help when help was needed. —*God Calling*, edited by A. J. Russell

☐ 320 _____

According to your faith, let it be to you. (Matthew 9:29, KJV)

TAKEAWAY

There is absolutely only one thing that can hinder the shepherd (Father), and that is, if the sheep will not trust Him and refuse to let Him take care of them.

No sheep, could it talk, would say to the shepherd, "I long for the food you have provided and for the shelter and peace of your fold, and I wish I might dare to enjoy them, but alas! I feel

too unworthy. I am too weak and foolish; I do not feel grateful enough. I dare not presume to think you mean all these good things for me." One can imagine how grieved and wounded a good shepherd would be. —Hannah W. Smith, *The God of All Comfort*

□ 321 _____

God is our refuge and strength, a very present help in trouble. Therefore we will not fear though the earth should change, though the mountains shake in the heart of the sea; though its waters roar and foam, though the mountains tremble with its tumult. (Psalm 46:1-3, RSV)

TAKEAWAY
In every change, he faithful will remain.

□ 322 _____

The chariots of God are tens of thousands and thousands of thousands. Those who trust in the Lord are like Mount Zion, which cannot be shaken but endures forever. ❖ As the mountains surround Jerusalem, so the Lord surrounds his people both now and forevermore. (Psalms 68:17; 125:1-2, NIV)

TAKEAWAY
The Lord surrounds his people with tens of thousands of chariots both now and forevermore.

MIND MENDER: I have been driven many times to my knees by the overwhelming conviction that I had nowhere else to go. My own wisdom, and that of all about me, seemed insufficient for the day. —Abraham Lincoln

Forty-Seven

AM I JUST A FACE IN THE CROWD TO GOD?

☐ 323 _____

He himself has said, "I will never leave you nor forsake you." ❖ Lord . . . you are thinking about me constantly! I can't even count how many times a day your thoughts turn toward me. And when I waken in the morning, you are still thinking of me! (Hebrews 13:5, NKJV; Psalm 139:18)

TAKEAWAY
Lord, when I waken in the morning, you are still thinking of me!

☐ 324 _____

Before a word is on my tongue you know it completely, O Lord. You hem me in—behind and before; you have laid your hand upon me. Such knowledge is too wonderful for me, too lofty for me to attain. ❖You created my inmost being; you knit me together in my mother's womb. (Psalm 139:4-6, 13, NIV)

TAKEAWAY
I am on God's mind.

☐ 325 _____

Are not five sparrows sold for two pennies? Yet not one of them is forgotten by God. Indeed, the very hairs of your head are all numbered. Don't be afraid; you are worth more than many sparrows. (Luke 12:6-7, NIV)

TAKEAWAY
I used to imagine God hidden behind a fat book or a newspaper or taking a nap when I came near to talk to him in prayer because that is how I remember my own beloved but imperfect father, who loved to read or doze in his favorite chair. Sometimes, Dad seemed unapproachable. But God is the *perfect* Father, and I am his cherished child whom he deems worthy of his undivided attention at all times.
—Anonymous

☐ 326 _____

Long ago, even before he made the world, God loved us and chose us in Christ to be holy and without fault in his eyes. ❖Isn't he your Father who created you? Has he not made you and established you? ❖ Even when I walk through the dark valley of death, I will not be afraid, for you are close beside me. Your rod and your staff protect and comfort me. ❖ Surely your goodness and unfailing love will pursue me all the days of my life. (Ephesians 1:4; Deuteronomy 32:6; Psalm 23:4, 6)

TAKEAWAY

You think about people, but God thinks about you. —Leo Tolstoy, *Last Diaries*

O Lord, you have examined my heart and know everything about me. You know when I sit down or stand up. You know my every thought. (Psalm 139:1-2)

☐ 327 _____

Because of what Christ has done, we have become gifts to God that he delights in. ❖ For the Lord your God . . . will rejoice over you with great gladness. With his love, he will calm all your fears. He will exult over you by singing a happy song. (Ephesians 1:11; Zephaniah 3:17)

TAKEAWAY

I think that if you and I had just one tenth of the joy in having God that He has in having us as His children, we would explode with joy! Imagine—if God brought the universe into being with simply a word, can we even begin to grasp what God's shouts of joy over us must be like? —David Needham, *Birthright*

All those who love me will do what I say. My
Father will love them, and we will come to them
and live with them. ❖Do not be afraid, for I am
with you. ❖I will guide you along the best path-
way for your life. I will advise you and watch over
you. (John 14:23; Isaiah 43:5; Psalm 32:8, NKJV)

T A K E A W A Y
Do not be afraid, for I am with you.

☐ 329

O Lord, you have searched me and you know me.
You know when I sit and when I rise; you perceive
my thoughts from afar. You discern my going out
and my lying down; you are familiar with all my
ways. (Psalm 139:1-3, NIV)

T A K E A W A Y
O Lord, you know when I sit and when I rise.

MIND MENDER: God has made his children by adop-
tion nearer to himself than the angels. The angels are
the friends of Christ; believers are his members.
—Thomas Watson, *The Golden Treasury of Puritan Quotations*

Forty-Eight

BIRTHRIGHT:
WHO AM I?

☐ 330 _____

For God knew his people in advance, and he
chose them to become like his Son, so that his
Son would be the firstborn, with many brothers
and sisters. And . . . he called them to come to
him. And he gave them right standing with himself, and he promised them his glory. ❖ So now
Jesus and the ones he makes holy have the same
Father. That is why Jesus is not ashamed to call
them brothers and sisters. ❖ As we know Jesus better, his divine power gives us everything we need
for living a godly life. He has called us to receive
his own glory and goodness! He has promised . . .

that you will share in his divine nature. (Romans 8:29-30; Hebrews 2:11; 2 Peter 1:3-4)

God knew his people in advance, and he chose them. He gave them right standing with himself.

☐ 331 _____

The Lord has set apart the godly for himself. (Psalm 4:3)

Dear One:
You are mine.
—God

☐ 332 _____

Those who become Christians become new persons. They are not the same anymore, for the old life is gone. A new life has begun! ❖ We can understand these things, for we have the mind of Christ. (2 Corinthians 5:17; 1 Corinthians 2:16)

Few Christians today have a grasp on the fact that their inner man delights in the law of God! —David Needham, *Birthright*

God is love. God is my Father. Therefore, since I have *his* genes, there is the ability and desire to love in *my* genes.

Then God said, "Let us make people in our image, to be like ourselves. They will be masters over all life—the fish in the sea, the birds in the sky, and all the livestock, wild animals, and small animals." So God created people in his own image; God patterned them after himself; male and female he created them. God blessed them and told them, "Multiply and fill the earth and subdue it. Be masters over the fish and birds and all the animals." ❖Then God looked over all he had made, and he saw that it was excellent in every way. (Genesis 1:26-28, 31)

TAKEAWAY

So you should not be like cowering, fearful slaves. You should behave instead like God's very own children, adopted into his family— calling him "Father, dear Father." For his Holy Spirit speaks to us deep in our hearts and tells us that we are God's children. And since we are his children, we will share his treasures. (Romans 8:15-17)

Your enjoyment of the world is never right till every morning you awake in Heaven; see yourself in your Father's palace. —Thomas Traherne

TAKEAWAY

Of all the marvelous aspects of the human body, I know of no greater wonder than that every one of the hundred trillion cells in my body has access to the brain. —Dr. Paul Brand, *Fearfully and Wonderfully Made*

Look in a mirror and marvel at God's creation, a work of art—YOU! Open your hands, palms up. Think about the wonder of your fingerprints—the only ones like that among the billions of people in the world.

☐ 334 _____

But when the right time came, God sent his Son, born of a woman, subject to the law. God sent him to buy freedom for us who were slaves to the law, so that he could adopt us as his very own children. And because you . . . have become his children, God has sent the Spirit of his Son into your hearts, and now you can call God your dear Father. Now you are no longer a slave but God's own child. And since you are his child, everything he has belongs to you. (Galatians 4:4-7)

T A K E A W A Y
You are richer than you think.

☐ 335 _____

Know ye not that ye are the temple of God, and that the Spirit of God dwelleth in you? (1 Corinthians 3:16, KJV)

T A K E A W A Y
Deep within the heart abides identity. It either paces the heart's floor in search of discovery or rests in confidence, having been discovered.
—Preston Gillham, *Lifetime Guarantee* magazine

When I look at the night sky and see the work of your fingers—the moon and the stars you have set in place—what are mortals that you should think of us, mere humans that you should care for us? For you made us only a little lower than God, and you crowned us with glory and honor. ❖ It has pleased God to tell his people that the riches and glory of Christ are for you . . . too. For this is the secret: Christ lives in you, and this is your assurance that you will share in his glory. ❖ You are the salt of the earth. (Psalm 8:3-6; Colossians 1:27; Matthew 5:13)

TAKEAWAY

When I take on Christ's spirit of love (a holy spirit), then I become the salt of the earth, seasoning that makes living tolerable for myself and other people.

MIND MENDER: When we accept Christ, God immediately gives us special recognition, status, authority, power and a host of privileges. If we are ignorant of these, we will dutifully plod through life quite certain that Christianity isn't all that it is supposed to be.
—Erwin Lutzer, *You're Richer Than You Think*

Forty-Nine

LOOKING AHEAD

☐ 337 _____

Eye has not seen, nor ear heard, nor have entered into the heart of man the things which God has prepared for those who love him. (1 Corinthians 2:9, NKJV)

TAKEAWAY
While on this earth we are on the wrong side of the door. All the leaves of the New Testament are rustling with the rumor that it will not always be so. —C. S. Lewis

☐ 338 _____

Just as we are now like Adam, the man of the earth, so we will someday be like Christ, the man from heaven. . . . Let me tell you a wonderful secret God has revealed to us. Not all of us will die, but we will all be transformed. It will happen in a moment, in the blinking of an eye, when the last trumpet is blown. For when the trumpet sounds, the Christians who have died will be raised with transformed bodies. And then we who are living will be transformed so that we will never die. ❖ How we thank God, who gives us victory over sin and death through Jesus Christ our Lord! So, my dear brothers and sisters, be strong and steady, always enthusiastic about the Lord's work, for you know that nothing you do for the Lord is ever useless. (1 Corinthians 15:49-52, 57-58)

TAKEAWAY

> *Thro' many dangers, toils and snares*
> *I have already come.*
> *'Tis grace hath bro't me safe thus far,*
> *And grace will lead me home.*
>
> *When we've been there ten thousand years,*
> *Bright, shining as the sun,*
> *We've no less days to sing God's praise*
> *Than when we first begun.*

—*JOHN NEWTON, "Amazing Grace"*

☐ 339 _____

He will swallow up death in victory; and the Lord God will wipe away tears from off all faces; and the rebuke of his people shall he take away from off all the earth. ❖ Nation shall not lift up a sword against nation, neither shall they learn war any more. (Isaiah 25:8; Micah 4:3, KJV)

Every morning, lean thine arms awhile upon the window-sill of Heaven, and gaze upon the Lord . . . then, with that vision in thy heart, turn strong to meet the day. —Unknown

☐ 340 _____

Listen to me, dear brothers and sisters. Hasn't God chosen the poor in this world to be rich in faith? Aren't they the ones who will inherit the kingdom God promised to those who love him? ❖ He will remove all of their sorrows, and there will be no more death or sorrow or crying or pain. For the old world and its evils are gone forever. ❖ "All who are victorious will inherit all these blessings, and I will be their God, and they will be my children." (James 2:5; Revelations 21:4, 7)

God is in control. He is moving history toward a climax.

☐ 341 _____

Jesus told her, "I am the resurrection and the life. Those who believe in me, even though they die like everyone else, will live again. They are given eternal life for believing in me and will never perish." ❖ For God has reserved a priceless inheritance for his children. It is kept in heaven for you, pure and undefiled, beyond the reach of change and decay. (John 11:25-26; 1 Peter 1:4)

For God has reserved a priceless inheritance for his children. They are given eternal life for believing in Jesus.

☐ 342 _____

Since you have been raised to new life with Christ, set your sights on the realities of heaven, where Christ sits at God's right hand in the place of honor and power. Let heaven fill your thoughts. Do not think only about things down here on earth. For you died when Christ died, and your real life is hidden with Christ in God. And when Christ, who is your real life, is revealed to the whole world, you will share in all his glory. ❖ So be truly glad! There is wonderful joy ahead, even though it is necessary for you to endure many trials for a while. (Colossians 3:1-4; 1 Peter 1:6)

TAKEAWAY
There is wonderful joy ahead, even though it is necessary for you to endure many trials for a while.

☐ 343 _____

So be on your guard, not asleep like the others. Stay alert and be sober. ❖ Continue to live in fellowship with Christ so that when he returns, you will be full of courage and not shrink back from him in shame. ❖ But the day of the Lord will come as unexpectedly as a thief. ❖ But we are looking forward to the new heavens and new earth he has promised, a world where everyone is right with God. ❖ Dear brothers and sisters, you must be patient as you wait for the Lord's return. Consider the farmers who eagerly look for the rains in the fall and in the spring. They patiently wait for the precious harvest to ripen. ❖ Job is an example of a man who endured patiently. From his experience we see how the Lord's plan finally ended in good, for he is full of tenderness and mercy. (1 Thessalonians 5:6; 1 John 2:28; 2 Peter 3:10, 13; James 5:7, 11)

TAKEAWAY
"Surely I am coming quickly." Amen. Even so, come, Lord Jesus. (Revelation 22:20, NKJV)

MIND MENDER: The prophetic Scriptures give us "hope." Without Scripture's plan of God for the future and the hope it brings, I do not know what the average thinking person does. Certainly a person will not find the answer by wringing his hands, or by committing suicide, or by turning to the occult. We find the answer to the future in Holy Scripture. It is summed up in the person of Jesus Christ. God has centered all our hopes and dreams on Him. He is the Commander-in-Chief of these angelic armies that will accompany Him on His return. —Billy Graham, *Angels*

Fifty

WHEN THERE IS A DECISION TO MAKE

☐ 344 _____

Fools think they need no advice, but the wise listen to others. ❖The godly give good advice to their friends; the wicked lead them astray. ❖The advice of the wise is like a life-giving fountain; those who accept it avoid the snares of death. (Proverbs 12:15, 26; 13:14)

TAKEAWAY
The wise listen to others.

☐ 345 _____

Commit your work to the Lord, and then your plans will succeed. ❖The Lord despises pride; be assured that the proud will be punished. . . . It is better to be poor and godly than rich and dishonest. We can make our plans, but the Lord determines our steps. . . . The Lord demands fairness in every business deal; he sets the standard. ❖People may think they are doing what is right, but the Lord examines the heart. The Lord is more pleased when we do what is just and right than when we give him sacrifices. ❖Never let loyalty and kindness get away from you! Wear them like a necklace; write them deep within your heart. Then you will find favor with both God and people, and you will gain a good reputation. Trust in the Lord with all your heart; do not depend on your own understanding. Seek his will in all you do, and he will direct your paths. (Proverbs 16:3, 5-11; 21:2-3; 3:3-6)

TAKEAWAY
Commit your work to the Lord, and then your plans will succeed.

☐ 346 _____

Thy word is a lamp unto my feet, and a light unto my path. ❖Thou through thy commandments hast made me wiser than mine enemies. . . . I have more understanding than all my teachers; for thy testimonies are my meditation. I understand more than the ancients, because I keep thy precepts. . . . How sweet are thy words unto my taste! yea, sweeter than honey to my mouth! Through thy precepts I get understanding. (Psalm 119:98-105, KJV)

God is *not* silent. He has spoken in the Bible. When we exclaim in frustration, "However can I get God to speak to me?" we forget that he *has* spoken through his Word; yes, through that very Bible lying on your coffee table or standing on end on your bookshelf! What God has said is sufficient for today's living. We need only to look to the Bible. His Word stands *yesterday, today, and forever.*

□ 347 _____

Reverence for the Lord is the foundation of true wisdom. The rewards of wisdom come to all who obey him. ❖ To you, O Lord, I lift up my soul. ❖ Show me the path where I should walk, O Lord; point out the right road for me to follow. ❖ The Lord is good and does what is right; he shows the proper path to those who go astray. ❖ Turn to me and have mercy on me, for I am alone and in deep distress. ❖ Let me not be put to shame, O Lord, for I have cried out to you. (Psalms 111:10; 25:1, 4, 8, 16; 31:17, NIV)

The Lord is good and does what is right; he shows the proper path to those who go astray.

□ 348 _____

I am but a foreigner here on earth; I need the guidance of your commands. Don't hide them from me!

❖At midnight I rise to thank you for your just laws. (Psalm 119:19, 62)

Thy will be done. (Matthew 6:10, KJV)

☐ 349 _____

Tune your ears to wisdom, and concentrate on understanding. . . . Search for them as you would for lost money or hidden treasure. Then you will understand what it means to fear the Lord, and you will gain knowledge of God. For the Lord grants wisdom! From his mouth come knowledge and understanding. He grants a treasure of good sense to the godly. . . . He guards the paths of justice and protects those who are faithful to him. Then you will understand what is right, just, and fair, and you will know how to find the right course of action every time. (Proverbs 2:1-9)

T A K E A W A Y
The Lord grants a treasure of good sense to the godly.

☐ 350 _____

If any of you lack wisdom, let him ask of God, that giveth to all men liberally, and upbraideth not; and it shall be given him. But let him ask in faith, nothing wavering. For he that wavereth is like a wave of the sea driven with the wind and tossed. (James 1:5-6, KJV)

Solomon could have asked for anything, but he asked for wisdom so he might know how to do the job God had given him to do.

MIND MENDER: Let everyone who is godly pray to Thee in a time when Thou mayest be found.

I will instruct you and teach you in the way which you should go; I will counsel you with My eye upon you.

So I advise you to live according to your new life in the Holy Spirit. Then you won't be doing what your sinful nature craves.

If we are living now by the Holy Spirit, let us follow the Holy Spirit's leading in every part of our lives. Let us not become conceited, or irritate one another, or be jealous of one another. —Psalm 32:6, 8, NASB; Galatians 5:16, 25-26

Fifty-One

WHEN FORGIVING SOMEONE IS DIFFICULT

☐ 351 _____

Put on therefore, as the elect of God, holy and beloved, bowels of mercies, kindness, humbleness of mind, meekness, longsuffering; forbearing one another, and forgiving one another, if any man have a quarrel against any: even as Christ forgave you, so also do ye. (Colossians 3:12-14, KJV)

TAKEAWAY

To hate someone is to allow that person a large measure of control over my emotions and feelings, which are then held hostage to that hated individual's behavior. Forgiveness will free me from that bondage. The only cure for bitterness is remembering that Christ freed me from all judgment and gave me forgiveness without condemnation. Because he did it, I will do it.

224

God blesses those who are merciful, for they will
be shown mercy. ❖If your enemies are hungry,
give them food to eat. If they are thirsty, give them
water to drink. You will heap burning coals on
their heads, and the Lord will reward you. (Matthew 5:7; Proverbs 25:21-22)

TAKEAWAY

**Everyone says forgiveness is a lovely idea until
they have something to forgive.** —C. S. Lewis

We have a great high priest . . . Jesus the Son of
God. Ours is not a high priest unable to sympa-
thize with our weaknesses, but one who, because
of his likeness to us, has been tested every way,
only without sin. Let us therefore boldly approach
the throne of our gracious God, where we may . . .
find timely help. (Hebrews 4:14-16, NEB)

TAKEAWAY

**Jesus knew all about betrayal. He invested
three years of his life teaching his disciples—
including Judas. He did miracles before their
eyes and even washed his disciples' feet—
including Judas's. Then Judas turned traitor
for thirty pieces of silver. When Jesus pre-
dicted his own betrayal (John 13:18), he
quoted another person who knew what it was
like to have a friend turn on him: David.
Despite Judas's despicable betrayal, Jesus
asked forgiveness at the cross on behalf of**

not only his executioners but Judas and all the rest of us. His words were, "Father, forgive them, for they do not know what they do" (Luke 23:34, NKJV). However could he manage to utter those words while nailed there to the cross, his body bleeding and in excruciating pain? What love!

The King of kings and Lord of the entire universe is now able to identify with us, his most lowly subjects, when we have been wronged and when forgiveness comes hard for us. He knows. He understands.

☐ 354 _____

See that none render evil for evil unto any man; but ever follow that which is good, both among yourselves, and to all men. ❖ Not rendering evil for evil, or railing for railing: but contrariwise blessing; knowing that ye are thereunto called, that ye should inherit a blessing. ❖ There is laid up for me the crown of righteousness, which the Lord, the righteous Judge, will give to me on that Day [of his appearing]. (1 Thessalonians 5:15; 1 Peter 3:9, KJV; 2 Timothy 4:8, NKJV)

TAKEAWAY

And so throughout eternity
I forgive you, you forgive me;
As our dear Redeemer said,
This is the Wine, this is the Bread.

—WILLIAM BLAKE

All have sinned and fall short of the glory of God. ❖ Why do you see the speck that is in your brother's eye, but do not notice the log that is in your own eye? Or how can you say to your brother, "Let me take the speck out of your eye," when there is the log in your own eye? (Romans 3:23; Matthew 7:3-4, RSV)

T A K E A W A Y

> *Lord make me an instrument of your peace.*
> *Where there is hatred, let me sow love;*
> *Where there is injury, pardon;*
> *Where there is doubt, faith;*
> *Where there is despair, hope;*
> *Where there is darkness, light;*
> *Where there is sadness, joy.*
>
> —PRAYER OF ST. FRANCIS OF ASSISI

You have heard that it was said, "You shall love your neighbor and hate your enemy." But I say to you, Love your enemies and pray for those who persecute you, so that you may be sons of your Father who is in heaven; for he makes his sun rise on the evil and on the good, and sends rain on the just and on the unjust. ❖ For if you love those who love you, what reward have you? Do not even the tax collectors do the same? And if you salute only your brethren, what more are you doing than others? Do not even the Gentiles do the same?

You, therefore, must be perfect, as your heavenly Father is perfect. (Matthew 5:43-48, RSV)

TAKEAWAY
He calls us to attempt what we previously thought impossible. He presses us into challenges that demand far greater power from him than we've ever known. He shows us a life we've never dreamed we could live.

We are like sailboats tossing in a restless sea, waiting for a stiff, bracing wind to fill our sails and get us moving according to the Master's charts and toward his goals. He takes our breath away with his soul-sized challenges and with his offer to accomplish them through us. The "hard sayings" of Jesus confront us with the other half of the Gospel—the alarming, amazing and awesome potential entrusted to us as followers of Christ. —Lloyd J. Ogilvie, *The Other Jesus*

☐ 357 _____

If I hate or despise any one man in the world, I hate something that God cannot hate, and despise that which he loves. And though many people may appear to us ever so sinful, odious, or extravagant in their conduct, we must never look upon that, as the least motive for any contempt or disregard of them; but look upon them with the greater compassion, as being in the most pitiable condition that can be. —William Law

Father, forgive them; for they know not what they do. (Luke 23:34, KJV)

MIND MENDER: Just as bitterness produces more bitterness in others, so love begets love. Love cures people—both the ones who give it and the ones who receive it. —Alan Loy McGinnis and Karl Menninger

Fifty-Two

I CAN DO ALL THINGS THROUGH HIS STRONG, WONDERFUL, MAJESTIC, TRUSTWORTHY NAME

Today's name for God: My Rock

☐ 358 _____

The Lord is my rock and my fortress and my deliverer; my God, my rock, in whom I take refuge; my shield and the horn of my salvation, my stronghold and my refuge; my savior, Thou dost save me from violence. (2 Samuel 22:2-3, NASB)

TAKEAWAY

The Lord is my rock and my fortress in whom I take refuge.

I have been to the bottom pits of life, and I can tell you with absolute certainty that our God, the Rock, is there too. He was the fortress that I ran to through it all, and he was sufficient. —Young husband whose wife was killed in a traffic accident

Today's name for God: My Hope

☐ 359 _____

We exult in hope of the glory of God . . . ❖ and
hope does not disappoint, because the love of
God has been poured out within our hearts
through the Holy Spirit who was given to us. ❖
And may the God of hope fill you with all joy and
peace in believing, that you may abound in hope
by the power of the Holy Spirit. ❖ Why are you in
despair, O my soul? And why are you disturbed
within me? Hope in God, for I shall again praise
Him, the help of my countenance, and my God.
❖ Be strong and let your heart take courage, all
you who hope in the Lord. (Romans 5:2, 5; 15:13;
Psalms 43:5; 31:24, NASB)

TAKEAWAY
He is the God of hope.

O Lord, our Lord, how majestic is Thy name
in all the earth. (Psalm 8:1, KJV)

Today's name for God: A Defense for the Helpless

☐ 360 _____

To the poor, O Lord, you are a refuge from the
storm. To the needy in distress, you are a shelter
from the rain and the heat. For the oppressive acts
of ruthless people are like a storm beating against
a wall. ❖ The Israelites . . . groaned beneath their
burden of slavery. They cried out for help, and
their pleas for deliverance rose up to God. ❖ He
looked down on the Israelites and felt deep concern for their welfare. ❖ And that very day the Lord

began to lead the people of Israel out of Egypt, division by division. (Isaiah 25:4; Exodus 2:23, 25; 12:51)

Lord, thanks that you really are a refuge from the storms in my life, a cool shadow from the overheated pace of my life, a shelter from the distressing, driving rains that invade the circumstances of my life.

Today's name for God: My Helper

☐ 361 _____

Save me, O God, by Thy name, and vindicate me by Thy power. . . . Give ear to the words of my mouth. For strangers have risen against me, and violent men have sought my life. . . . Behold, God is my helper; the Lord is the sustainer of my soul. ❖Willingly I will sacrifice to Thee; I will give thanks to Thy name, O Lord, for it is good. For he has delivered me from all trouble. ❖The unfortunate commits himself to Thee. . . . The Lord is King forever and ever. . . . O Lord, Thou hast heard the desire of the humble; Thou wilt strengthen their heart, Thou wilt incline Thine ear to vindicate the orphan and the oppressed. ❖In the Lord I take refuge. (Psalms 54:1-4, 6-7; 10:14-18; 11:1, NASB)

> *Immortal, invisible, God only wise,*
> *In light inaccessible hid from our eyes,*
> *Most blessed, most glorious, the Ancient of Days,*
> *Almighty, victorious, Thy great name we praise.*

We blossom and flourish as leaves on the tree,
And wither and perish—but naught changeth
thee.

—WALTER CHALMERS SMITH, *"Immortal, Invisible, God Only Wise"*

Today's name for God: The One Who Lifts My Head
☐ 362 _____

O Lord, how my adversaries have increased! Many
are rising up against me. Many are saying . . .,
"There is no deliverance for him in God." But
Thou, O Lord, art a shield about me, my glory,
and the One who lifts my head. I was crying to the
Lord with my voice, and He answered me from
His holy mountain. I lay down and slept; I awoke,
for the Lord sustains me. I will not be afraid of ten
thousands of people who have set themselves
against me round about. Arise, O Lord; save me, O
my God! For Thou hast smitten all my enemies
on the cheek; Thou hast shattered the teeth of the
wicked. Salvation belongs to the Lord. (Psalm 3:1-
8, NASB)

TAKEAWAY
**Thou, O Lord, art a shield about me, the One
who lifts my head.**

Today's name for God: My Hiding Place
☐ 363 _____

Let everyone who is godly pray to Thee in a time
when Thou mayest be found. . . . Thou art my hiding place; Thou dost preserve me from trouble;
Thou dost surround me with songs of deliverance.

❖He who trusts in the Lord, lovingkindness shall surround him. Be glad in the Lord and rejoice. (Psalm 32:6-7, 10-11, NASB)

TAKEAWAY
Thou art my hiding place.

Today's name for God: Faithful One

☐ 364 _____

No temptation has overtaken you but such as is common to man; and God is faithful, who will not allow you to be tempted beyond what you are able, but with the temptation will provide the way of escape also, that you may be able to endure it. ❖If we are unfaithful, he remains faithful, for he cannot deny himself. (1 Corinthians 10:13, NASB; 2 Timothy 2:13)

TAKEAWAY
God will not allow you to be tempted beyond what you are able.

Today's name for God: My Shepherd
☐ 365 _____

I am the good shepherd; the good shepherd lays down His life for the sheep. He who is a hireling, and not a shepherd, who is not the owner of the sheep, beholds the wolf coming, and leaves the sheep, and flees, and the wolf snatches them, and scatters them. He flees because he is a hireling, and is not concerned about the sheep. I am the good shepherd; and I know My own, and My own know Me, even as the Father knows Me and I know the Father; and I lay down My life for the sheep. ❖ My sheep hear My voice, and I know them, and they follow Me; and I give eternal life to them, and they shall never perish; and no one shall snatch them out of My hand. (John 10:11-15, 27-28, NASB)

MIND MENDER: I know the Good Shepherd, and each day his voice becomes more familiar and comforting to me.